Book **H**

Specific Skill Series

Identifying Inferences

William H. Wittenberg

Fifth Edition

D0874401

SRA/McGraw-Hill
Columbus, Ohio

Cover, Back Cover, John Downer/Masterfile

SRA/McGraw-Hill

A Division of The McGraw·Hill Companies

Send all inquiries to:
    SRA/McGraw-Hill
    8787 Orion Place
    Columbus, OH 43240-4027

ISBN 0-02-688008-3

        6 IPC 02 01

To the Teacher

PURPOSE:

IDENTIFYING INFERENCES is designed to develop one of the most difficult interpretive skills—arriving at a *probable* conclusion from a limited amount of information. IDENTIFYING INFERENCES requires the readers to *read between the lines*. They must utilize previously acquired knowledge and past experiences in order to fully comprehend the message of the text.

FOR WHOM:

The skill of IDENTIFYING INFERENCES is developed through a series of books spanning ten levels (Picture, Preparatory, A, B, C, D, E, F, G, H). The Picture Level is for pupils who have not acquired a basic sight vocabulary. The Preparatory Level is for pupils who have a basic sight vocabulary but are not yet ready for the first-grade-level book. Books A through H are appropriate for pupils who can read on levels one through eight, respectively. **The use of the *Specific Skill Series Placement Test* is recommended to determine the appropriate level.**

THE NEW EDITION:

The fifth edition of the *Specific Skill Series* maintains the quality and focus that has distinguished this program for more than 25 years. A key element central to the program's success has been the unique nature of the reading selections. Nonfiction pieces about current topics have been designed to stimulate the interest of students, motivating them to use the comprehension strategies they have learned to further their reading. To keep this important aspect of the program intact, a percentage of the reading selections have been replaced in order to ensure the continued relevance of the subject material.

In addition, a significant percentage of the artwork in the program has been replaced to give the books a contemporary look. The cover photographs are designed to appeal to readers of all ages.

SESSIONS:

Short practice sessions are the most effective. It is desirable to have a practice session every day or every other day, using a few units each session.

SCORING:

Pupils should record their answers on the reproducible worksheets. The worksheets make scoring easier and provide uniform records of the pupils' work. Using worksheets also avoids consuming the exercise books.

It is important for pupils to know how well they are doing. For this reason, units should be scored as soon as they have been completed. Then a discussion can be held in which pupils justify their choices. (The Integrated Language Activities, many of which are open-ended, do not lend themselves to an objective score; thus there are no answer keys for these pages.)

GENERAL INFORMATION ON *IDENTIFYING INFERENCES*:

The difference between a *conclusion* and an *inference*, as presented in this series, is that a conclusion is a logical deduction based upon conclusive evidence, while an inference is an "educated guess" based upon evidence that is less than conclusive. Read this sample:

> Captain Fujihara quickly parked the fire truck, grabbed his helmet, and rushed into the house at 615 Oak Street.

You can *conclude* that Captain Fujihara knows how to drive because that ability was required to park the fire truck. You can *infer* that there is a fire at 615 Oak Street because Captain Fujihara took his helmet and rushed into that house. This is an inference because firefighters do rush to put out fires. It is an inference because there may be another reason for the firefighter's rushing to the house. Captain Fujihara may live there and be late for supper. Thus an inference is supported by evidence, but the evidence is not necessarily conclusive.

SUGGESTED STEPS:

1. Pupils read the text. On levels C-H, after reading, pupils examine the statements that follow the text to determine whether each is a factually true statement (T), a false statement (F), or a valid inference (I). ("True" statements are those about which the reader can be *certain* from the text.) On lower levels, pupils determine which statement about the text or picture is probably true.
2. Then pupils reexamine the text or picture for evidence to support their decisions.
3. Pupils record their answers on the worksheets.

RELATED MATERIALS:

Specific Skill Series Placement Tests, which enable the teacher to place pupils at their appropriate levels in each skill, are available for the Elementary (Pre-1–6) and Midway (4–8) grade levels.

About This Book

In a story, a writer does not tell the reader everything. A careful reader is able to make educated guesses about things the author does not tell. An educated guess is a guess that is based on facts the author provides plus the reader's own knowledge and experience. For example, an author may write the following in a story:

> Harry clutched a handkerchief tightly in his fingers. Sobbing, he raised his hand to wipe away the tears that trickled down his cheeks.

You can make an educated guess that Harry is sad, based on the fact that he is crying and on your own knowledge that people sometimes cry when they are sad.

This kind of educated guess is called an **inference**. You cannot be *certain* that your inference is correct. In the example above, Harry may be crying because he has hurt himself. Or he may be crying because he is very happy. Other details in the story will help you make the best possible guess.

In this book, you will read short stories. Then you will read four sentences about each story. You will have to decide whether each sentence is true (T), false (F), or an inference (I). A true statement tells a fact from the story. A false statement is one that is not true. An inference says something that is *probably* true based on facts in the story and your own knowledge and experience. More than one sentence about one story may be true, false, or an inference. You must read each sentence carefully to decide which it is.

1. "Do you know the answer to this math problem, Gordon?" asked Mrs. Reyes. Gordon shook his head. He hadn't done his homework.

"I'll try to help you understand the problem," said Mrs. Reyes, "since you didn't get your homework done."

"My older brother had you for a teacher two years ago, and he had problems with math, too," said Gordon.

"Your brother and you are alike," said Mrs. Reyes. "Maybe you can try to set aside a special time to study in your home."

---

2. "Luke Fisher is one of the most talented basketball players I've ever seen," said Judy.

"He's not particularly talented," Tim disagreed. "He's just tall. That gives him an unfair advantage over others. If he were only six feet four inches, he wouldn't be considered outstanding."

"His height gives him an advantage," said Judy, "but I wouldn't call it unfair. Plenty of tall people are terrible basketball players."

"Answer this question then," said Tim. "Is Fisher as dominant since he graduated as he was in that game against Berner High?"

"No, I must admit that since he's playing against better competition, he's not as outstanding," said Judy. "But he's still very good."

---

3. Did you know that the hanging gardens of Babylon were actually one large pyramid? Long ago, King Nebuchadnezzar II of Mesopotamia had each level of a large pyramid planted with flowers and trees to create the effect of a colorful hillside. He did this to please his wife, whose homeland was green and hilly. These gardens are included among the Seven Wonders of the World.

---

4. The driver of the special tractor-bus announced, "We are now on the surface of the glacier." The Wilson family and other tourists stepped down gingerly onto the ice.

"This glacier is really a river of ice moving down the valley a few feet a year," declared their guide. "The spot on which we're standing will take over 250 years to reach the bottom and melt." Just then Billy Wilson's camera fell into a deep crack in the glacier.

---

5. "This toothache has been bothering me for days," complained Stan.

"Why don't you see your dentist?" advised Terry.

"I'd rather put up with pain than see the dentist," replied Stan.

"If I were you," said Terry, "I wouldn't put off going."

"But I'm afraid of what my dentist will say," Stan frowned. "I may have to spend hours having cavities drilled and filled."

"The longer you wait," said Terry, "the more you'll suffer when you do go. If you delay too long, you may lose all your teeth!"

			T	F	I
1.	(A)	Gordon's brother had had Mrs. Reyes for a teacher.	☐	☐	☐
	(B)	Mrs. Reyes wanted to help Gordon understand the math problem.	☐	☐	☐
	(C)	Both Gordon and his brother have poor study habits.	☐	☐	☐
	(D)	Mrs. Reyes did not remember Gordon's brother.	☐	☐	☐

			T	F	I
2.	(A)	Judy is a loyal fan of Luke Fisher.	☐	☐	☐
	(B)	Luke Fisher played very well against Berner High.	☐	☐	☐
	(C)	Luke Fisher is less than six feet four inches tall.	☐	☐	☐
	(D)	Tim doesn't think Luke Fisher is especially talented.	☐	☐	☐

			T	F	I
3.	(A)	The gardens contained flowers and trees.	☐	☐	☐
	(B)	The hanging gardens grew on a hillside.	☐	☐	☐
	(C)	King Nebuchadnezzar II had the gardens built for his own pleasure.	☐	☐	☐
	(D)	The landscape around the gardens was quite flat.	☐	☐	☐

			T	F	I
4.	(A)	Billy's camera will not be found for at least 250 years.	☐	☐	☐
	(B)	The Wilsons were not the only tourists on the tractor-bus.	☐	☐	☐
	(C)	Ordinary buses cannot go on glaciers.	☐	☐	☐
	(D)	Billy fell into a crack in the glacier.	☐	☐	☐

			T	F	I
5.	(A)	Terry advised Stan to go to the dentist.	☐	☐	☐
	(B)	Terry has probably had experience in postponing dental work.	☐	☐	☐
	(C)	Stan is afraid of what his dentist will say.	☐	☐	☐
	(D)	Stan's toothache began an hour ago.	☐	☐	☐

1.   Laura was writing in her diary when she heard the lookout cry, "Thar she blows!" Laura rushed from her cabin to the ship's rail. Near the ship a great whale lifted out of the water. Laura gazed in wonder at the huge animal. Usually Laura did not have much to write about in her diary. Today, however, she wrote a description of the whale: "The whale's head is as big as four whole rooms, and his body as long as our ship."

2.   Lissa, a sophomore in college, is working her way through school by holding a series of part-time jobs. Two days a week she works as a cashier in the college bookstore. Lunch hours usually find her at the campus store, where she works behind the counter. During the weekends, Lissa works as a waitress at a popular restaurant in town. Despite so many hours at work, Lissa is a conscientious student who makes *A*s and *B*s in all her subjects.

3.   Crack! The gun sounded in the crisp, cold air. Like a bullet, skier number 14 zoomed out of the starting gate, her face set with determination as she attacked the slope with a vengeance. Faster and faster she flew, her body bent low, her whiplike turns leaving a cloud of snow in her trail. The crowd cheered as she swooped to a stop at the bottom of the mountain, her breath coming in quick gasps, a smile lighting her flushed face.

4.   "I see there was an accident here," remarked Helen, slowing the car and peering over the steering wheel. "Look at all that debris in the road, Ann." Bits of glass and shiny slivers of metal glittered on the road ahead. As the car moved forward, the tires made a crunching sound. Helen increased the car's speed. It began to shudder and bump unevenly. Helen drew off to the side of the road and brought the limping vehicle to a halt.

5.   Thelma gazed out the window with the most forlorn look Jessie had ever seen. Thelma was one of her best friends, and it hurt Jessie to see that sad expression on Thelma's face. Jessie was determined to help. "I'll have to think of something," Jessie said to herself. In a moment, an idea came to her. "I'll ask Caroline to come over. She's helped Thelma and me so many times."

		T	F	I

1. (A) Laura was in her cabin when the lookout cried out. ☐ ☐ ☐
   (B) Laura had previously filled her diary with stories just as exciting. ☐ ☐ ☐
   (C) Laura had never been this close to a large whale before. ☐ ☐ ☐
   (D) Laura wrote that the whale's body was as long as the ship. ☐ ☐ ☐

		T	F	I

2. (A) Lissa is working her way through school. ☐ ☐ ☐
   (B) Lissa is a senior in college. ☐ ☐ ☐
   (C) A restaurant employs Lissa as a waitress. ☐ ☐ ☐
   (D) Lissa is an energetic person. ☐ ☐ ☐

		T	F	I

3. (A) The skier has completed a successful run in competition. ☐ ☐ ☐
   (B) A cloud of snow was left in the skier's trail. ☐ ☐ ☐
   (C) The skier got off to a fast start. ☐ ☐ ☐
   (D) The skier kept her knees straight and her body erect. ☐ ☐ ☐

		T	F	I

4. (A) Not all the debris from the accident had been cleared away. ☐ ☐ ☐
   (B) The car got a flat tire from driving over the debris. ☐ ☐ ☐
   (C) Helen pulled off the road and stopped the car. ☐ ☐ ☐
   (D) Helen was driving alone in the car. ☐ ☐ ☐

		T	F	I

5. (A) Caroline can usually raise the spirits of Thelma and Jessie. ☐ ☐ ☐
   (B) Jessie couldn't bear to see Thelma in low spirits. ☐ ☐ ☐
   (C) Thelma and Jessie are very good friends. ☐ ☐ ☐
   (D) Jessie couldn't think of an idea for helping Thelma. ☐ ☐ ☐

1.   Dr. Harriet Bern was pleased that she had gained so many patients in such a short period of time. But as time passed and more and more people came to her for treatment, she found that she was unable to take care of everyone. To find another doctor to help her, Dr. Bern placed an announcement in a medical journal. Within a few weeks, many other doctors called Dr. Bern to offer their help.

2.   For many years, Mrs. Alvarez had successfully planted beets, cucumbers, carrots, and squash in a small garden near her house. This year, she decided to take her friend's advice. She would make her vegetables grow even larger than they had grown before by using a costly fertilizer and by watering the plants more often. After she had applied the fertilizer and watered the plants frequently for two weeks, Mrs. Alvarez noted that the vegetables had not increased significantly in size.

3.   Because Martha had never before played in a championship softball game, she was very tense and nervous. During the early innings, she made three errors and struck out. But then Martha noticed that her parents were smiling and cheering her on from their seats in the stands. As the game progressed, Martha felt much calmer. By the seventh inning, the young athlete was no longer making errors and had gotten several base hits.

4.   "I wonder how blue jeans got their name," mused Victor.
      "I just read about that," responded Michelle. "The pants were first made for sailors in the Italian port of Genoa. The name *jeans* came from the French word for *Genoa*, or *Gênes*," said Michelle. "Also, the cloth for the pants came from the French town of *Nîmes*. In French, *de* means 'from' or 'of,' and the name *denims* came from *de Nîmes*," added Michelle.

5.   Simone felt that the car she was driving gave her too much trouble. Because her repair bills were very high, she considered buying a new car. After shopping for two weeks, Simone discovered that she would have to spend at least $7,000 for the car she wanted. She knew that if she spent $7,000, she would have to give up her summer vacation. Simone then took her old car to a different mechanic, who promised to make it run like new for $2,500. Simone felt much better after she heard that.

UNIT 3

			T	F	I
1.	(A)	Dr. Bern had gained an excellent reputation.	☐	☐	☐
	(B)	Dr. Bern placed an announcement in a medical journal.	☐	☐	☐
	(C)	The response to Dr. Bern's announcement was poor.	☐	☐	☐
	(D)	Dr. Bern had gained more patients than she could handle.	☐	☐	☐

			T	F	I
2.	(A)	Initially, Mrs. Alvarez believed her friend to be an authority on gardening.	☐	☐	☐
	(B)	Mrs. Alvarez had planted vegetable gardens for many years.	☐	☐	☐
	(C)	Mrs. Alvarez will go back to her own methods of gardening.	☐	☐	☐
	(D)	The fertilizer suggested by Mrs. Alvarez' friend was inexpensive.	☐	☐	☐

			T	F	I
3.	(A)	The presence and reassuring behavior of Martha's parents had a positive effect on her.	☐	☐	☐
	(B)	The softball game was a championship game.	☐	☐	☐
	(C)	Martha made three errors during the early innings.	☐	☐	☐
	(D)	Martha made a base hit early in the game.	☐	☐	☐

			T	F	I
4.	(A)	The first blue jeans were made to withstand hard work.	☐	☐	☐
	(B)	Blue jeans were named after a French sailor.	☐	☐	☐
	(C)	*Denims* came from a phrase meaning "from Nîmes."	☐	☐	☐
	(D)	Italian people used goods only from Italy.	☐	☐	☐

			T	F	I
5.	(A)	Simone did not buy a new car.	☐	☐	☐
	(B)	Simone spent two months shopping for a new car.	☐	☐	☐
	(C)	A new car would cost Simone $2,500.	☐	☐	☐
	(D)	Simone's repair bills had been costly.	☐	☐	☐

1.   "I'm sorry I'm late, but the clock in the library was behind time and I didn't notice. The custodian said the electric power had been off for a while." Liz dumped her books on the table and sat down breathlessly.

"It's okay, Liz," said Peggy. "At least you did get here and we can study for that test tomorrow." She looked at her watch. "We have another hour left before I have to leave."

---

2.   "This house isn't quaint," complained Tom. "It's just plain run-down. I wish we had gone to look at the new ranch house Mrs. Tate described. That's more my style."

"Oh, come on," said his wife Margo. "Have a little imagination. Think of how we can fix this place up."

"Fix me up, you mean," replied her husband. "I'd probably fall off a ladder the first day!"

---

3.   Lori sat staring into space and drumming her fingers on the counter. "Look, Lori," her mother finally said, "if you don't have anything to do, why don't you call Cheryl and Diane? Maybe you could all go skating together."

"No way," Lori answered. "The basketball championships are tonight. Everyone in the Pep Club will be spending the whole day decorating the school gym."

---

4.   "I can't believe it, Sam," said Nita. "Are you really staying home this summer?"

"That's right," Sam said. "I'll be right here all summer."

"What?" asked Cory. "You mean you're not going to camp?"

"That's right," Sam answered.

"And you're not going on a cruise with your grandmother? Or taking a car trip with your mom?" Judy asked.

"Or going on one of your famous bus trips?" Sara continued.

"Right," said Sam again, "I'm not going anywhere this summer."

---

5.   The expression "That's not worth peanuts" was probably not used by the great American scientist George Washington Carver. While doing plant research, Carver discovered that peanut crops could make Southern farm soil fertile. To encourage farmers to plant peanuts, Carver created over three hundred uses for peanuts in manufactured goods such as ink and soap. His inventions brought new life to farming in the South.

		T	F	I
1.	(A) Liz does not wear a watch.	☐	☐	☐
	(B) Peggy and Liz have an hour left for studying.	☐	☐	☐
	(C) The clock in the library kept good time.	☐	☐	☐
	(D) Liz said she was sorry to be late.	☐	☐	☐

		T	F	I
2.	(A) Margo wants to buy a house to fix up.	☐	☐	☐
	(B) Mrs. Tate is a real estate agent.	☐	☐	☐
	(C) Tom says the house is "just plain run-down."	☐	☐	☐
	(D) Margo wants to buy a ranch house.	☐	☐	☐

		T	F	I
3.	(A) Cheryl and Diane belong to the Pep Club.	☐	☐	☐
	(B) The basketball championships are tonight.	☐	☐	☐
	(C) Lori's mother suggested that Lori call Cheryl and Diane.	☐	☐	☐
	(D) Lori does not belong to the Pep Club.	☐	☐	☐

		T	F	I
4.	(A) Nita said she couldn't believe that Sam was staying home this summer.	☐	☐	☐
	(B) Sam told the four girls that he would be away for the summer.	☐	☐	☐
	(C) Judy asked Sam if he were going on a cruise with his grandmother.	☐	☐	☐
	(D) Sam usually goes away during the summer.	☐	☐	☐

		T	F	I
5.	(A) Carver discovered that peanut crops could make Southern soil more fertile.	☐	☐	☐
	(B) As a result of Carver's inventions, peanuts became more useful.	☐	☐	☐
	(C) Until Carver's inventions, peanuts were used only as food.	☐	☐	☐
	(D) Peanuts led to the failure of farming in the South.	☐	☐	☐

1.　"Did you find what you were looking for?" asked Mr. Whiting.

　　"Yes, thanks, I did," answered Robin. "I'm getting ideas for a party from this book, *Happy Birthday Parties*, by Penny Warner. It tells about different ways to celebrate a birthday. In fact, twenty different themes are suggested. Since my birthday's in June, I'm going to try an outdoor sleepover party."

2.　"Alma's coming to visit today," Mrs. Beebe told Nurse Kelly. "I like Alma so much, but I do wish she'd make up her mind about marrying that boyfriend of hers. Alma and Marvin have dated each other for five years now. It's getting monotonous!" At that moment, Marvin and Alma walked in. Alma looked nervous as she twisted something on her left hand. The once-timid Marvin was puffed up like a frog and wore an enormous grin. Nurse Kelly winked at them both.

3.　"I just read about some real buried treasure," said Lee.

　　"Really? Where is it and how did it get there?" asked Dana.

　　"It is believed to be on the Island of Cocos, off the coast of Costa Rica. In 1821, some Spanish gold fell into the hands of an English sea captain. He quickly sailed for Cocos and buried the treasure there. No one has found it yet," explained Lee.

4.　"It's impossible for me to get up today," groaned Ben. "My eyes seem to be rolling around in my head. I'm terribly dizzy and weak. My stomach is upset, too."

　　"You have the same symptoms I started with," replied Abigail. "It's not just a twelve-hour virus, either. It may be a week or more before you feel better. Just stay in bed and rest until the dizziness goes away and you feel hungry again. Then eat lightly and drink plenty of liquids. You'll eventually get your strength back."

5.　This was going to be a special Christmas for the Monroe family. In the past they had always spent the holiday by themselves in their New Hampshire home. This year, however, their cousins, the Burroughs, had planned to visit. It would be the first time Rachel had ever met her younger cousin Valerie. "Do you think Valerie will like New Hampshire?" asked Rachel.

　　"I think she'll be excited to see the snow," replied Mrs. Monroe.

		T	F	I

1. (A) This conversation took place in the library.
    (B) Robin was planning to have a party in the basement rec room.
    (C) Penny Warner had written a book of ideas for birthday parties.
    (D) Mr. Whiting is a librarian.

		T	F	I

2. (A) Mrs. Beebe doesn't like Alma.
    (B) Formerly, Marvin had appeared shy and afraid.
    (C) Mrs. Beebe requires nursing care.
    (D) Alma and Marvin have agreed to marry.

		T	F	I

3. (A) The sea captain planned to come back for the treasure but never did.
    (B) The treasure has been buried for only fifty years.
    (C) The gold is believed to be on the Island of Cocos.
    (D) No one has yet found the treasure.

		T	F	I

4. (A) Abigail told Ben to eat three big meals a day.
    (B) Abigail had been sick for a week or more.
    (C) Ben had an upset stomach.
    (D) Ben didn't feel well enough to get up.

		T	F	I

5. (A) It never snows where Valerie lives.
    (B) Rachel and Valerie had never met before.
    (C) The Monroe family planned to visit the Burrough family.
    (D) In the past the Monroes had always spent Christmas by themselves.

1.   "Let's run down to the beach and do our exercises there," suggested Tara. "We'd better put our sneakers on, after what happened to Tony."

"But I love the way the sand feels on my bare feet," said Sue.

Tara frowned. "The problem is that there could be broken glass hidden just under the top layer of sand. It's not a risk worth taking."

"You're right," said Sue. "The last thing I need is a bad cut on my foot. I'll put on sneakers, just as you're doing."

---

2.   "I'm exhausted," gasped Mark. "I'm dropping out of the race!"

"Come on," encouraged Diane. "The finish line is just ahead."

"It may seem near to you, but I might as well be running across the Sahara Desert." Mark slowed down to a walk. His chest heaved beneath his sweat-soaked shirt. "I can't make it," he said.

"Oh!" cried Diane. "The finish line is only three miles away."

"Three miles!" cried Mark. "I thought you said the finish line was just ahead. This will be the last marathon I ever run in—the very last!"

---

3.   The gas station was being held up! A robber was pointing a gun at the employees, who put their hands up, trembling with fear.

Seeing all this happen, Kerry ran to a phone booth and called the police. "There's a robbery taking place at the gas station at Grand Avenue and Merrick Road," she shouted into the phone.

"No robbery is taking place there," said the police dispatcher calmly.

"What do you mean?" asked Kerry frantically.

"A movie is being made at that location," laughed the dispatcher. "The robber you saw was an actor with a fake gun. Thanks for calling, though. If that had been a real robbery, we'd have been right there."

---

4.   Donald couldn't take the test. He hadn't studied, and he knew he'd fail if he took it. "I'm sick to my stomach," he lied. "I'd better go home."

The teacher said he could take the test tomorrow.

Donald went home and cried. He was so upset that he couldn't study. That night he got very little sleep.

When Donald took the test the next day, he was tired and really did feel a little sick. Donald failed the test and felt miserable for days.

---

5.   "I'm looking forward to my train trip across the country," said Mr. Matheson.

"I can't understand why anyone would travel by train," said Mrs. Banks. "A plane gets you there many times faster."

"That may be true," replied Mr. Matheson, "but traveling by train is more relaxing for me. I enjoy seeing the countryside."

"I don't have that much time, and I don't enjoy the sights," said Mrs. Banks. "I need to get where I'm going by plane as fast as I can."

UNIT 6

			T	F	I
1.	(A)	Tara suggested exercising on the beach.	☐	☐	☐
	(B)	While on the beach, Tony had cut his foot on glass.	☐	☐	☐
	(C)	Sue disliked the feeling of sand on her bare feet.	☐	☐	☐
	(D)	Tara explained that broken glass can lie just below the sand's surface.	☐	☐	☐

			T	F	I
2.	(A)	Mark said he was dropping out of the race.	☐	☐	☐
	(B)	Diane tried to encourage Mark to keep going.	☐	☐	☐
	(C)	Diane was in better condition than Mark.	☐	☐	☐
	(D)	Diane said the finish line was only two miles away.	☐	☐	☐

			T	F	I
3.	(A)	Kerry couldn't see the cameras and movie equipment from the phone booth.	☐	☐	☐
	(B)	The police dispatcher scolded Kerry for calling.	☐	☐	☐
	(C)	The actors had succeeded in making the fake robbery look real.	☐	☐	☐
	(D)	The gas station being filmed was on the corner of Maple and Grove Streets.	☐	☐	☐

			T	F	I
4.	(A)	The teacher told Donald he could take the test tomorrow.	☐	☐	☐
	(B)	Donald felt guilty about lying and pretending to be sick.	☐	☐	☐
	(C)	Donald became too upset to study or sleep.	☐	☐	☐
	(D)	Donald passed the test the next day.	☐	☐	☐

			T	F	I
5.	(A)	Mrs. Banks prefers plane to train travel.	☐	☐	☐
	(B)	Mr. Matheson likes to relax and see the countryside.	☐	☐	☐
	(C)	Mr. Matheson is looking forward to his trip to China.	☐	☐	☐
	(D)	Mrs. Banks has a busy schedule to maintain.	☐	☐	☐

"This house isn't haunted," said Jan. "It's just plain creepy. But I wish we hadn't come here in the middle of the night like this. I'd rather be home listening to the new tape I bought today."

"Come on," said Lee. "It's Halloween, and maybe we'll see a ghost. Let's go upstairs and take a quick look around."

"Oh, Lee," answered Jan looking back anxiously, "this is silly. Who believes in ghosts, for goodness' sake?"

A. Exercising Your Skill

The passage above tells about two girls in a scary house on Halloween. Stories sometimes take place during holidays or special days. In your reading, you will see how holidays or special days can affect characters and the situations they are in. Each holiday has specific symbols associated with it. Holidays are often connected with special feelings or moods, too. Characters are affected by these feelings and moods.

Sometimes holidays and their effects are described directly in a story, but sometimes they are only suggested. Even if you and your family do not celebrate these holidays, you probably know enough about them to recognize the special things that are connected with them. Practice recognizing the symbols and moods of some commonly celebrated holidays by playing the following word-association game with a partner. One partner should read the sentences in the first paragraph, stopping at each blank.

The other partner should say a word to complete each blank. Change roles for the second paragraph.

1. On Thanksgiving Day, my family _____ . We eat _____ and _____ . We give thanks for _____ . At school I learn about how the _____ helped the _____ survive during their first year in a new land. Thanksgiving makes me feel _____ .

2. On Halloween, I usually sew my own _____ . I _____ with my friends. Everything seems more _____ on Halloween night. I seem to see _____ hiding everywhere. Lighted _____ with cut-out faces do not help very much either.

B. Expanding Your Skill

Continue associating symbols and feelings with holidays. Read each group of words or phrases below. On your paper, write the best heading for each group.

1. resolutions, beginning, noisemakers, midnight, hopefulness
2. flags, parades, fireworks, liberty
3. hearts, flowers, cards, cupid, love
4. green, shamrocks, leprechauns, Irish
5. Santa Claus, evergreen trees, stockings, holly, giving

C. Exploring Language

Read the following passages, and answer the questions on your paper. Some of the answer information will be directly stated in the passage, and some will be suggested.

1.	Marita dug deep in her purse, searching for more change. She knew that Cassie would treasure a leather-bound copy of *Little Women*, and Marita had just found one. "This is the season for giving," thought Marita, "and I'll give this to her if I possibly can!"

	a.	Why was Marita searching for more change?
	b.	Were Marita and Cassie good friends?
	c.	Was Cassie with Marita when this event took place?
	d.	What holiday season was it?
	e.	What was special about the copy of *Little Women* that Marita had found?

2.	"I just won a lottery, and I'm going to share the money with all my friends," announced Mark. Suddenly Mark was surrounded by people he barely knew, declaring their undying friendship. "The joke's on you!" laughed Mark as he walked quickly away from the crowd, chuckling to himself. This was his favorite day of the year—a day when he was actually allowed to play tricks on people!

	a.	What did Mark say he was going to share with his friends?
	b.	Did Mark really win a lottery?
	c.	Were the people around Mark really his friends?
	d.	It was probably what holiday?
	e.	Did Mark think the crowd of people would be angry with him?

D. Expressing Yourself

Choose one of these activities.

1.	Write a letter to a pen pal in a foreign country. In the letter, describe what you did on a holiday that your pen pal doesn't celebrate in his or her country. (Only the United States celebrates Independence Day on July 4th, for example.) Give some direct information about the holiday. Use indirect details to give hints about your feelings and reactions to the holiday. Ask a classmate to read your letter and comment on how well you communicated the feeling of the holiday.

2.	With a group of classmates, play Holiday Grab. Write the names of several holidays on slips of paper, and put the slips in a box or a bag. Take turns choosing a holiday and acting it out without words. Use body motions and facial features to act out symbols and feelings associated with the holiday. See how quickly your classmates can guess it.

UNIT 7

1.   Once upon a time there was a horse who grazed in a special pasture. One day, a stag came along and said that he had as much right to graze in the pasture as the horse did. Wanting to be rid of the stag, the horse asked a man to help him. The man said that he would help, but to do so he must put a bridle in the horse's mouth and ride on his back. The horse agreed, and the two of them ran the stag out of the pasture. Once the stag was gone, however, the bridled and mounted horse realized that he had gotten rid of the stag only to lose his freedom.

2.   The triathlon is an exhausting race that involves long-distance swimming, biking, and running, in that order. Carla was training to take first place.

"If you intend to win this," her coach instructed, "you need to make far better time than the others in the biking and running sections of the race."

3.   Many friends came to see Janet in the school play. When it was her time to appear, Janet walked confidently to the middle of the stage. Then she saw all the people. She became frightened and momentarily forgot her lines. But when she saw her friend Linda in the audience, Janet decided to pretend that she was talking to Linda as she said her lines. From then on, it was easier for her to remember the part.

Afterward, many people told Janet what a great job she had done. "Some day you'll be a famous actress," they said.

"I don't think I ever want to get up on a stage again," said Janet.

4.   "There's a rattlesnake living in your cellar," said Larry.

"Rattlesnakes often hibernate there," said Grandpa. "Some spend the summer in the cellar to escape the heat."

"Why do you let poisonous snakes live there?" asked Larry.

"Somehow they always seem to find their way there," said Grandpa.

"Can't you get rid of them?" asked Larry.

"Yes, but others would take their places," said Grandpa. "Anyway, at least I know where they are. And besides, the rattlesnakes eat little animals that would otherwise be eating plants in my garden."

5.   "There's a big, green, evil-looking bug on a bush in the yard," said Tod. "If it stays there, I'll get rid of it. . . permanently!"

"Before you do anything," said Grandma, "let's have a look."

Tod and Grandma walked over to the bush.

"Look!" said Grandma, "It's laying eggs right on this bush."

"Oh, dear!" said Tod, "I should have acted when I first saw it."

"Nonsense!" said Grandma. "This insect looks frightening, but it's harmless. It even eats other bad insects. It's called a praying mantis."

			T	F	I
1.	(A)	The horse wanted to get rid of the stag.	☐	☐	☐
	(B)	The man had a selfish reason for helping the horse.	☐	☐	☐
	(C)	The stag thought that the pasture belonged to the horse.	☐	☐	☐
	(D)	The man had become the horse's new master.	☐	☐	☐

			T	F	I
2.	(A)	Carla's weakest point was her swimming.	☐	☐	☐
	(B)	In the triathlon, swimming comes first.	☐	☐	☐
	(C)	Carla was training to finish the race, not to win it.	☐	☐	☐
	(D)	The coach knew Carla's strengths and weaknesses.	☐	☐	☐

			T	F	I
3.	(A)	Janet didn't become frightened until she was actually in front of the audience.	☐	☐	☐
	(B)	Seeing a friend in the audience helped Janet control her fears.	☐	☐	☐
	(C)	No one spoke to Janet after the play was over.	☐	☐	☐
	(D)	Many friends of Janet attended the play.	☐	☐	☐

			T	F	I
4.	(A)	Grandpa explained that rattlesnakes eat other garden pests.	☐	☐	☐
	(B)	Larry was concerned about the harm the rattlesnakes could do.	☐	☐	☐
	(C)	Grandpa didn't know that rattlesnakes spent time in his cellar.	☐	☐	☐
	(D)	Grandpa said that some rattlesnakes live in the cellar to escape the heat.	☐	☐	☐

			T	F	I
5.	(A)	Grandma told Tod the name of the insect.	☐	☐	☐
	(B)	Tod would have killed a harmless creature if Grandma hadn't stopped him.	☐	☐	☐
	(C)	The praying mantis was laying eggs on the ground.	☐	☐	☐
	(D)	Tod described the insect as "big, green, and evil-looking."	☐	☐	☐

1.   Arthur held the steering wheel tightly. He was very nervous, but he tried to look relaxed and confident. He tried not to look at the somber stranger in the front seat with him who was taking notes as Arthur drove. Arthur looked into the rear-view mirror, signaled, and put the car into reverse gear. He thought things had gone better this time. All he had to do now was to back the car safely into the parking place. Arthur waited as another motorist passed him, and then he began backing up. The car fit nicely into the space.

2.   Jonathan and Jan had been married just a few weeks, and they were buying their first new car. Jonathan's eyes kept going back to the little two-seater in the center of the showroom. It reminded him of an expensive Italian sports car, but it was American and did not cost as much. But Jan was firm. "It's just too small for us," she said. "It may be a great second car, but this is our first." Jonathan sighed as he slid behind the steering wheel of a compact sedan. He could see the little two-seater through the windshield. Jan sat beside him, smiling.

3.   Whitney had been looking forward to her first day at Carver Academy for the last two years. She felt this would be the most exciting day of her life. She had planned her every move and anticipated her every need in order to be certain this would be the start of a perfect high-school career. It was important to her that she look her best, so, to that end, Whitney convinced her mother that new clothes were the order of the day. But when she and her mother returned home from their shopping spree and opened the boxes, looks of astonishment crossed their faces.

4.   "Keep them below," ordered Captain Harley. "I want no one on deck but ordinary sailors. Our ship must look like a peaceful trading vessel. Now, let's hoist all sails and raise the British flag."
        Harley's ship, the *Avenger*, began closing in on a large British merchant vessel. Soon, the two were sailing side by side. "Now!" shouted Captain Harley. The crew poured onto the deck. The vessels were almost touching when Captain Harley ordered the British flag lowered and the flag with the skull and crossbones raised.

5.   Lee stared at the wall. A small space still looked bad. Should she go back and repaint it? But if she did that, she would lose time. She would also have to clean the brush again. Lee groaned. She wanted to go to a party later, and it would take her the rest of the afternoon to get ready. Maybe her neighbor wouldn't notice the badly painted area. Lee sighed. Then she pulled the paint can toward her and slipped the screwdriver under the lid.

		T	F	I
1.	(A) The examiner seemed more like a friend than a stranger.	☐	☐	☐
	(B) Arthur had failed the test previously.	☐	☐	☐
	(C) Arthur tried to keep his anxiety from showing.	☐	☐	☐
	(D) Arthur will pass his driver's test this time.	☐	☐	☐

		T	F	I
2.	(A) As a bachelor, Jonathan would have bought the two-seater.	☐	☐	☐
	(B) Jan couldn't take her eyes off the sports car.	☐	☐	☐
	(C) The sports car had been made in America.	☐	☐	☐
	(D) Jonathan and Jan will buy the compact sedan.	☐	☐	☐

		T	F	I
3.	(A) Carver Academy is a two-year junior college.	☐	☐	☐
	(B) Whitney's mother went shopping with Whitney.	☐	☐	☐
	(C) What was in the boxes was not what they had ordered.	☐	☐	☐
	(D) Whitney wanted to get new clothes that were becoming to her.	☐	☐	☐

		T	F	I
4.	(A) At first, Harley wanted the *Avenger* to look like a British trading vessel.	☐	☐	☐
	(B) The *Avenger* carried a crew of pirates.	☐	☐	☐
	(C) At the end, Harley ordered his crew to raise the skull and crossbones.	☐	☐	☐
	(D) The British ship closed in on the *Avenger*.	☐	☐	☐

		T	F	I
5.	(A) Lee could repaint the space quickly.	☐	☐	☐
	(B) Lee would have to clean her brush if she repainted the area.	☐	☐	☐
	(C) Lee will repaint the area on the wall.	☐	☐	☐
	(D) Lee wondered if her neighbor would notice the badly painted area.	☐	☐	☐

1.   "I can't defend you," said the lawyer. "Please take your case elsewhere."

"What do you mean you can't defend me?" shouted the man. "You're supposed to be good at getting people out of trouble."

"Yes, I'm good at getting people out of trouble, but you're in a little too much trouble," answered the lawyer.

"Wait a second," said the man angrily, "I'll pay you well. This is an outrage. You're supposed to be on my side."

"I can't take your case," repeated the lawyer. "You'll undoubtedly lose in court. I don't like to lose."

---

2.   Detective Langley knelt and carefully examined the body's many knife wounds. Then she noticed a fragment of thin cardboard clutched in the sprawled victim's hand. Two unused matches hung from it, and on it was printed "Rainbow Di . . ." but the rest had been ripped away.

"Get over to the Rainbow Diner right away," Langley told two officers. "See if anyone remembers a bald man with a red beard eating there tonight. Get a description of anyone he was seen leaving with."

---

3.   "The yellow jackets are ruining our picnic," cried Mr. Conrad. "I don't like them on our food, and I don't care to get stung by them."

"I may have a solution," said Mrs. Conrad. She got honey and put it into a dish. Then she added water and sprinkled sugar over the mixture. She set the dish down a short distance away.

Soon all the yellow jackets had left the picnic table and had gone to the dish with the honey mixture.

"Thanks for saving our picnic," Sue said to her mother. "That's a good trick to know when you're eating outdoors in the summer."

---

4.   Elva switched the car's windshield wipers to high speed as the snow descended more heavily.

"I think we'd better stop for the night at a motel in this village," her friend Inez advised.

"But if we stop now, we'll miss skiing early tomorrow morning," said Elva. She gave the car more gas. It skidded briefly, then lurched up the road toward the mountains.

---

5.   Farming on the side of a mountain is no easy task, but that is what the early Inca people of the Andes Mountains had to do. For planting surfaces, the Incas built long, narrow, steplike banks of soil in the steep mountain slopes. Low stone walls supported these terraces, or *andennes*. Here, the Incas grew crops such as corn, potatoes, and cotton with water supplied by irrigation channels. This unique farming technique served the Incas well.

		T	F	I

1.
- (A) The man was willing to pay the lawyer well.
- (B) Preliminary evidence received by the lawyer had confirmed the man's guilt.
- (C) The lawyer told the man to come back another day.
- (D) The lawyer decided to take the case.

2.
- (A) The cardboard was part of a matchbook from the Rainbow Diner.
- (B) The victim had been stabbed with a knife more than once.
- (C) The victim was the bald, red-bearded man.
- (D) All the matches on the cardboard had been used.

3.
- (A) Yellow jackets are attracted to food, but they like sweets better.
- (B) Sue thanked her mother for saving the picnic.
- (C) Mr. Conrad didn't want to get stung by the yellow jackets.
- (D) Mr. Conrad complained about ants on the food.

4.
- (A) The snowfall was getting lighter.
- (B) Inez advised stopping for the night in the village.
- (C) The women had originally planned to spend that night nearer to the ski area.
- (D) When Elva gave the car more gas, it skidded.

5.
- (A) *Andennes* were the highest peaks in the Andes.
- (B) Growing their own crops was essential to the Incas' survival.
- (C) The Incas supported their terraces with wood.
- (D) Irrigation systems provided water for the crops.

1.   In 1986, the state of Texas enjoyed a year-long celebration of its 150th birthday. Known as the Lone Star State, Texas has also been called the nation's least bashful state. It was on April 21, 1836, that Sam Houston defeated the Mexican general Santa Anna at the battle of San Jacinto. From then until 1845 (when it became a state), the Republic of Texas existed as a separate nation. Texas is the only U.S. state that was ever a republic prior to becoming a part of the United States of America.

2.   Pica, an illness marked by the craving and consuming of nonfood items, is more common than most people realize. Chalk, clay, dirt, paper, plaster, starch, and tinfoil are only a few things eaten by people afflicted with pica. Some pica sufferers crave their own hair, eating it by the handfuls until clumps of it form in their stomachs and surgery is required. Pica is very common among children, who usually outgrow the condition by the time they reach five or six. Because young children often eat paint chips, laws have been designed to limit the amount of lead in house paint.

3.   It was 1873. A hush fell over the crowd as the speaker, Matilda Joslyn Gage, continued: "Are women governed? Most certainly; they pay taxes, they are held amenable to the laws; they are tried for crimes; they are fined, imprisoned, hung. The government wields strong power over them. Have they consented to this power of the government? Have they a recognized right to the ballot? Has their consent been asked through their votes? Have they had a voice in saying what taxes shall be levied on their property—what penalties they shall pay for crimes? *No.* They are ruled without their consent."

4.   Cassie and Daniel Sherman talked and shopped excitedly as they made plans for their trip home and their big surprise for their mother. Daniel bought paint, wallpaper, and blinds; Cassie paid for the new curtains, bedspreads, and towels. Together they purchased a new couch and an easy chair.

      Arrangements had been made for their mother, Mrs. Sherman, to visit her brother and his family for a few days. As soon as she left the shabby house, Daniel and Cassie moved their new purchases into it and set to work.

5.   The Fenno family were traveling through Pennsylvania, heading west, when Glenn suggested, "Let's watch for out-of-state license plates."

      "O.K." said Sally. "We'll make it a game with points. We're in Pennsylvania now, so Pennsylvania plates don't count at all."

      "There's an Ohio plate!" shouted Marie.

      "That's one point for you," said Sally. "A plate from Canada or Mexico counts for three points, and plates from Alaska or Hawaii count five points."

      "I'll keep score on this pad," offered Glenn.

1. (A) Texans take pride in being bold and adventuresome.
   (B) Sam Houston defeated Santa Anna in 1836.
   (C) In 1986, Texas was two hundred years old.
   (D) Texas became a state in 1845.

   T   F   I

2. (A) Babysitters need to learn about pica.
   (B) Pica sufferers generally crave chocolate candy and ice cream.
   (C) Children with pica are susceptible to lead poisoning.
   (D) By the time children are five or six, they usually outgrow pica.

   T   F   I

3. (A) In her speech, Gage pointed out that women pay taxes.
   (B) Gage was a leader of women's voting rights.
   (C) Gage said women had a voice in saying what penalties they should pay for crimes.
   (D) Gage made a speech about women in 1873.

   T   F   I

4. (A) Cassie and Daniel planned to surprise their mother.
   (B) Mrs. Sherman's house was shabby.
   (C) Cassie and Daniel were preparing to redecorate their mother's house.
   (D) Daniel paid for all the purchases made.

   T   F   I

5. (A) The Fennos played a game while traveling.
   (B) Alaska and Hawaii plates are rarely seen in Pennsylvania.
   (C) Marie made up the rules of the game.
   (D) Glenn offered to keep score.

   T   F   I

1.   Sherlock Holmes knelt and peered intently through his magnifying glass. "Aha, Watson!" he cried as he plucked from the carpet several strands of long white hairs, stained with red. "You see, the victim was struck here, and her body was taken elsewhere. It would have been impossible for such a fragile person to struggle successfully against a husky attacker."

2.   "Oh, my!" said Mr. Holt. "I'm in the exact-change lane and don't have a quarter for the parkway toll." He began searching frantically.

"Don't panic," said Mrs. Holt. "I have two dimes."

"Two dimes are not enough!" cried Mr. Holt. "We must find another nickel. Oh, no, oh, no!" he moaned.

"Here's a nickel on the floor!" Walter shouted triumphantly.

"Thank you, Walter," said Mr. Holt as he threw the change into the basket. Mr. Holt breathed a sigh of relief as he drove away from the toll plaza. "Thank you for saving the day."

3.   "I'm going to play Ricky at chess this afternoon," said Angie. "I won't be too rough on him. I'll give him some hints on playing."

"You'd better watch yourself," cautioned Timothy. "Do you really think you're that good?"

"It's not that I think I'm so good. I just don't think Ricky knows how to play very well," answered Angie. "He even admitted that he lost the last time he played."

"Well," said Timothy, "I'm afraid you've been taken in. Ricky did lose the last game he played. That game, however, was for the state championship, and he almost won it."

4.   Aunt Polly told Tom he had to paint the fence. Tom made a face but started to paint. Then he saw his friends coming. He began to smile and whistle as he painted.

"Too bad you can't come play with us," said his friends.

"I don't want to," said Tom. "Painting is too much fun."

"It is?" said one friend. "Let me try."

"Me too," said the others.

Tom handed over the brushes and sat under a tree smiling.

5.   "I've found a great way to raise money for our club's fund drive," exclaimed Randy. "I take my wagon from door to door, and I ask people for all their empty soda cans and milk bottles. Then I get the five-cent deposit for each empty can or bottle that goes back to the store in my wagon. It amounts to a fortune!"

"What an excellent way to make money!" cried Joanne. "Too bad we weren't able to do that before this year. We ought to thank the state legislature."

UNIT 11

		T	F	I
1.	(A) Watson found the strands of hair in a chair.	☐	☐	☐
	(B) Holmes told Watson that the victim's body had been taken somewhere else.	☐	☐	☐
	(C) The victim was an elderly lady.	☐	☐	☐
	(D) The victim had suffered a blow to the head.	☐	☐	☐

		T	F	I
2.	(A) The parkway toll was twenty-five cents.	☐	☐	☐
	(B) Mr. Holt was very concerned about holding up the cars behind them.	☐	☐	☐
	(C) Walter found a quarter.	☐	☐	☐
	(D) Mrs. Holt is not as excitable as Mr. Holt.	☐	☐	☐

		T	F	I
3.	(A) Angie and Ricky had never played chess together.	☐	☐	☐
	(B) Timothy told Angie that Ricky had competed for the state championship.	☐	☐	☐
	(C) Because of Timothy's revelation, Angie would be unsure of herself in the upcoming game.	☐	☐	☐
	(D) Ricky had won the last game he played.	☐	☐	☐

		T	F	I
4.	(A) People like work if they think it's fun.	☐	☐	☐
	(B) Tom was told that he had to paint the fence.	☐	☐	☐
	(C) Tom tricked his friends into doing his job.	☐	☐	☐
	(D) Tom painted along with his friends.	☐	☐	☐

		T	F	I
5.	(A) Joanne liked Randy's way of making money.	☐	☐	☐
	(B) The people that Randy collects from can afford to donate the deposit money.	☐	☐	☐
	(C) Randy took the empty bottles back to the store in his car.	☐	☐	☐
	(D) This year the legislature passed a law requiring deposits on bottles and cans.	☐	☐	☐

1.   "I can remember when the family used to get together more often," commented Aunt Dorothy. "We always had huge Sunday dinners. Everybody had a wonderful time."

"Well," replied Aunt Denise, "we did meet more often years ago. But we didn't always have a wonderful time. I can remember quite a few violent family arguments at those gatherings. Of course, you never would admit to that."

"They weren't arguments, Denise," responded Aunt Dorothy with a smile. "They were just discussions of politics."

---

2.   The Taj Mahal, once described as "poetry in stone," is actually a tomb. The Emperor Shah Jahan of India ordered construction of the eight-sided white marble building in 1631 to honor his wife Mumtaz Mahal who had just died. It took 20,000 workers over 20 years to complete the construction of the tomb along with a long reflecting pool and an immense garden surrounding the area.

---

3.   Amelia looked forward to her family's upcoming visit to a large amusement park. At the park, she planned to go on the roller coaster and as many other rides as possible. Her younger brother Peter, however, felt differently. He just wanted to spend the day at the park's swimming pool.

The children's parents sat with them to help resolve the problem. "Let's talk about it," they said. "But just remember one thing. No matter what we do, we must all stay together for the entire day."

---

4.   Traffic poked along the now-darkening streets of the city as Manuel made his way uptown toward his apartment on Ninety-seventh Street. To his left, he could see a gloomy row of buildings that appeared to huddle together in misery. To his right, he observed the fuzzy outlines of the park that always seemed so bright and cheerful during the day.

Impressed by what he saw, Manuel thought about how interesting it was that familiar places seemed to change as day turned into night.

---

5.   Michael and Maude could not agree on the kind of furniture they wanted for their new apartment. Michael said that he liked modern furniture. Maude, on the other hand, preferred country-style furniture.

"May I make a suggestion?" said the man standing next to them. "I've helped many young people in my time. Why don't you talk to our interior decorator before you make your final decision?"

"That seems like a good idea," responded Maude.

UNIT 12

			T	F	I
1.	(A)	What Aunt Dorothy called "discussions of politics" were really violent family arguments.	☐	☐	☐
	(B)	The two aunts disagreed about what had happened at the earlier family gatherings.	☐	☐	☐
	(C)	The family used to meet at Sunday dinners.	☐	☐	☐
	(D)	Aunt Denise said they always had a wonderful time at the family gatherings.	☐	☐	☐

			T	F	I
2.	(A)	Shah Jahan had adored his wife.	☐	☐	☐
	(B)	The Taj Mahal was built for Mumtaz Mahal's enjoyment.	☐	☐	☐
	(C)	The Taj Mahal is located in India.	☐	☐	☐
	(D)	The Taj Mahal took more than 20 years to build.	☐	☐	☐

			T	F	I
3.	(A)	Amelia and Peter were too young to be separated from their parents at the park.	☐	☐	☐
	(B)	Peter wanted to spend the day riding on the roller coaster.	☐	☐	☐
	(C)	Amelia was older than Peter.	☐	☐	☐
	(D)	The children's parents were unaware of the problem.	☐	☐	☐

			T	F	I
4.	(A)	Manuel usually traveled home during the day.	☐	☐	☐
	(B)	The traffic was moving swiftly.	☐	☐	☐
	(C)	Manuel was moving away from his apartment.	☐	☐	☐
	(D)	To his right, Manuel saw the park.	☐	☐	☐

			T	F	I
5.	(A)	The man who spoke to Michael and Maude was a salesman.	☐	☐	☐
	(B)	Michael likes Victorian furniture.	☐	☐	☐
	(C)	The man who spoke was older than Michael and Maude.	☐	☐	☐
	(D)	Maude agreed with the man who spoke.	☐	☐	☐

"Keep them below," ordered Captain Harley. "I want no one on deck but ordinary sailors. Our ship must look like a peaceful trading vessel. Now, let's hoist all sails and raise the British flag."

Harley's ship, the *Avenger*, began closing in on a large British merchant vessel. Soon, the two were sailing side by side. "Now!" shouted Captain Harley. The crew poured onto the deck. Their vessels were almost touching when Captain Harley ordered the British flag lowered and the flag with the skull and crossbones raised.

A. Exercising Your Skill

The passage above is about an event that took place during the age of piracy. There are many periods of history that have specific events, characteristics, people, symbols, or values associated ·with them. You will come across many historical periods in your reading. Information about a historical period may be specifically described in a story, or it may be suggested through details.

During various times, different things *motivated* people, or caused them to do what they did. For example, people who took part in the early colonization of America were probably motivated by the desire for religious freedom or for a better way of life.

Work with a small group of classmates to think about some of the things that motivate people. Come up with as many words or phrases as you can to describe the motivations of people during the time described.

The time of:
piracy   settling of the American or Canadian West
whaling boats   California or Yukon Gold Rush
early space exploration   Industrial Revolution

B. Expanding Your Skill

Continue thinking about details that could suggest different historical periods. Write the headings listed below on your paper. Find the words or phrases in the box that relate to each historical time, and write them under the heading. Use reference books to look up the words and phrases you don't know. Add other details you find that would fit under each heading.

Piracy, Whaling Boats, Early Space Exploration, Settling the West, California, Gold Rush, Industrial Revolution

skull and crossbones	prairie schooners	John Glenn
textile factories	satellites	boom towns
harpoons	Sutter's Mill	"Thar she blows!"
Sputnik	child labor	steam engines
sodbusters	Barbary coast	buccaneers
buried treasure	stake a claim	growth of cities

C. Exploring Language

Choose one of the time periods listed in Part B. Do additional research to find more details about it. Write two diary entries as if you were a character living during that time. Include some specific details that give information about the time. Also include some details that suggest what it was like to live during that time and what your feelings, values, and motivations might have been.

When you have finished writing, ask a classmate to read your entries. He or she should be able to answer some of the following questions from the information you have included or suggested.

Questions:

- What were some characteristics of the time?
- How did people get around then?
- What did people wear then? What did they eat?
- What did the imaginary writer of the diary do during a typical day?
- Was life generally easy or difficult for the writer?

_____
| _(Date)_____ |
| |
| *Dear Diary,* _____ |
| _____ |
| _____ |
| |
| _(Date)_____ |
| *Dear Diary,* _____ |
| _____ |
| _____ |
|_____|

D. Expressing Yourself

Choose one of these activities.

1. Pretend that you are a set director for a movie that will be set during a specific historical period. Write the name of the period and the title of the movie on your paper. Then, list props, costumes, and locations that will be used in the movie. Draw pictures of some of these if it would help to explain them. Next to some items, write notes telling how, where, or by whom they will be used.

2. In old magazines, find three or four pictures that show various time periods—or draw your own. Mount the pictures on paper, and write a descriptive caption for each. Combine your pictures with some classmates' pictures to make a "history scrapbook" to share with the rest of the class.

1.   "I can't wear any of these dresses to the party," cried Paula as she poked through her closet.

"Why not?" questioned her mother. "You have so many different styles of dresses to choose from."

Paula put her hands on her hips and turned toward her mother. "That's true," she agreed. "But they are the same styles that everyone else is wearing. For this party, I don't want to have that same look."

---

2.   Someone in the Jones house was playing music on the stereo system much too loudly. "That must be David," thought Mrs. Jones. "I'll just go upstairs and tell him to turn the volume down."

Mrs. Jones hurried to the upstairs den and opened the door. But instead of finding David listening to the music, she found her husband.

"John," she exclaimed with a smile, "if I had known you were here, I would have brought you a cup of coffee."

---

3.   Mary entered the fabric store and ordered three yards of material. "I want to make a tablecloth for my mom," she said.

"That's nice," chuckled the salesperson. "But what shape is the table? And what is its size?"

"The table is round. And it's twenty-four inches in diameter," explained Mary.

"If you buy just three yards of material," advised the salesperson, "you won't have enough. It takes more than four yards for a table that size."

---

4.   Born the daughter of former slaves, Mary McLeod valued education. In fact, Mary was the first in her family to learn to read. Mary went on to college and became a teacher. After marrying, Ms. McLeod and her husband moved to Florida where they found a large black population. Seeing a need, she decided to start a school for black children in Daytona Beach. Her school prospered and grew. In 1935, Mary McLeod Bethune was awarded the Spingarn Medal for contributing to the education of black people.

---

5.   The story of Amelia Earhart, the woman aviator who disappeared over the Pacific while trying to fly around the world in 1937, has been told many times. Earhart might never have reached fame or known the joy of flying had she not met Mrs. Neta Snook Southern. Southern, a pioneer of early aviation, gave Earhart flying lessons.

Before World War I, Southern built her own plane so she could learn to fly. She may have been the first woman pilot in the United States. Later, she began barnstorming and giving airplane rides and flying lessons to the public in California. One day a Mr. Earhart brought his daughter Amelia for a lesson. The rest is history.

UNIT 13

			T	F	I
1.	(A)	Paula is planning to go to a party.	☐	☐	☐
	(B)	Paula's mother pointed out that Paula had dresses of different styles.	☐	☐	☐
	(C)	Paula said she couldn't wear any of the dresses in her closet.	☐	☐	☐
	(D)	Paula and her mother will soon go shopping.	☐	☐	☐

			T	F	I
2.	(A)	Mrs. Jones doesn't criticize her husband for doing the same things she objects to the children doing.	☐	☐	☐
	(B)	Mrs. Jones gave Mr. Jones a cup of coffee.	☐	☐	☐
	(C)	Mr. Jones was listening to music in the upstairs den.	☐	☐	☐
	(D)	Music played too loudly usually irritates Mrs. Jones.	☐	☐	☐

			T	F	I
3.	(A)	Mary wanted to make a tablecloth for a square table.	☐	☐	☐
	(B)	Mary had little experience in making tablecloths.	☐	☐	☐
	(C)	The salesperson was skilled at measuring and selling fabrics.	☐	☐	☐
	(D)	The tablecloth was to be made for Mary's mother.	☐	☐	☐

			T	F	I
4.	(A)	There had been no school for black children in Daytona Beach before Ms. McLeod opened hers.	☐	☐	☐
	(B)	After receiving her own education, Ms. McLeod decided to become an educator herself.	☐	☐	☐
	(C)	Ms. McLeod came from a family of teachers.	☐	☐	☐
	(D)	Ms. McLeod recognized that education improves people's lives.	☐	☐	☐

			T	F	I
5.	(A)	Southern built her own plane before World War I.	☐	☐	☐
	(B)	Earhart took flying lessons from Southern.	☐	☐	☐
	(C)	Amelia Earhart was the first woman pilot in the United States.	☐	☐	☐
	(D)	Southern was an excellent teacher of flying.	☐	☐	☐

1.   The famous Swedish singer Jenny Lind once visited a home for the blind in Manchester, England. At first, she spent time just talking to the people, who had no idea who this kind lady was. After a while she asked them if they would like her to sing some of their favorite songs. As Lind sang the songs they knew and loved, they were deeply moved by her exquisite voice, so filled with feeling.

   "This must be Jenny Lind, 'the Swedish Nightingale,'" they whispered to one another excitedly.

---

2.   President Grover Cleveland preferred simple meals. Sometimes the fare at the White House was too fancy for his taste. One night he was attracted by the smell of a corned beef and cabbage dinner being cooked for the servants. He decided to trade his gourmet meal for theirs. Afterward the President declared that the boiled dinner was the best meal he had had in months.

---

3.   When George IV was to be crowned King of England, he tried to get rid of his wife, Caroline. First, he offered her a large sum of money if she would give up the right to call herself queen. When Caroline refused, George IV tried to prove that she was wicked and not fit to be his wife. This plan didn't succeed either. On the day of the coronation, Caroline went to Westminster Abbey demanding to be admitted and crowned as Queen of England. Soldiers kept her out. She turned away, broken-hearted. About three weeks later she died.

---

4.   "Are you happy you adopted me?" asked Alice. The family was gathered around the table celebrating Alice's eleventh birthday.

   "You must know that we are," said Father.

   "We couldn't love you any more than we do," added Mother.

   "I love you both, too," said Alice, "but I can't help wondering about my birth parents. Do you think they ever think about me on my birthday? Where did they come from, and why couldn't they keep me?"

   "It's natural for you to want to know the answers to those questions," said Father. "After we finish eating, we'll show you some pictures and letters."

---

5.   Most bathers had gone home when Carol decided to take one last swim in the lake. Her son Anthony was wading in shallow water near the shore. Swimming nearby was Priscilla, the pet pig of a friend. The pig was wearing a purple harness, its leash floating behind it.

   Suddenly Anthony got into water over his head and started to panic. Since the pig was closer to Anthony than Carol was, Carol yelled to her son to grab the pig's leash. Anthony did. After an initial struggle, Priscilla was able to drag Anthony toward shore until his feet touched the bottom once more.

UNIT 14

			T	F	I
1.	(A)	Jenny spent time talking to people at the home for the blind.	□	□	□
	(B)	The blind people knew that a voice of such superb quality must belong to a famous artist.	□	□	□
	(C)	Jenny Lind sang the songs the blind people knew and loved.	□	□	□
	(D)	Jenny Lind came from Sweden.	□	□	□

			T	F	I
2.	(A)	The corned beef and cabbage had been cooked for the servants.	□	□	□
	(B)	Grover Cleveland liked plain food.	□	□	□
	(C)	Corned beef and cabbage has an aroma that's easily detected.	□	□	□
	(D)	The corned beef and cabbage dinner got a poor rating from the President.	□	□	□

			T	F	I
3.	(A)	George IV had little love for his wife, Caroline.	□	□	□
	(B)	Caroline died about three months after the coronation.	□	□	□
	(C)	Caroline was more interested in prestige than money.	□	□	□
	(D)	George tried to prove that Caroline was wicked.	□	□	□

			T	F	I
4.	(A)	The truth about who she is is important to Alice.	□	□	□
	(B)	The family was celebrating Alice's eleventh birthday.	□	□	□
	(C)	Father and Mother refused to answer Alice's questions.	□	□	□
	(D)	Alice expressed hatred for her adoptive parents.	□	□	□

			T	F	I
5.	(A)	The pig wore a red harness.	□	□	□
	(B)	Anthony panicked when he got into deep water.	□	□	□
	(C)	Bathers had been at the lake earlier that day.	□	□	□
	(D)	Anthony couldn't swim.	□	□	□

1. "Class," began Ms. Michelson, "now that each group has chosen a foreign country to research and report on, take a few minutes to discuss your topic."

In Mimi's group, Vickie said, "I'd like to read about how the Eiffel Tower was built. Also, I think I read that there are some neat old castles in the southern part of France."

Lucas added, "I'm interested in that jet-powered Aerotrain."

"Well, I'd like to learn about French history," Mimi joined in.

---

2. Anyone with a poor sense of direction can buy a car with a navigation system on the dashboard. A flashing light shows where the car is headed. The car's location is set when the navigation mechanism is installed, and the mechanism keeps track from then on. Electronic sensing devices tell the car where it is. Navigation system maps on compact discs play in the same slot in which music compact discs play. One compact disc can hold a road map for about half the U.S.

---

3. Rhodes Scholarships for study at Oxford University in England are awarded with great prudence to outstanding college students around the world. One of the winners in 1985 has been not only an exemplary student but a champion skier. Bonnie Saint John of California was born with a defect that forced the amputation of her leg when she was five years old. Nevertheless, she won fourteen medals in national championships skiing on one leg and a bronze medal in the slalom and giant slalom at international games for the disabled in Innsbruck, Austria. Saint John, who received her bachelor's degree from Harvard University, chose politics as her major at Oxford.

---

4. Terry had a bad habit of going into Pat's room and taking things, such as paper or pencils, without asking. So it wasn't exactly surprising that, when Pat's money disappeared, Pat accused Terry of stealing.

"I didn't take your money!" Terry insisted angrily.

"But you always go into my room and take other things without asking," said Pat. "Who else would take it?"

Just then Mother came along. "When the paper carrier came I didn't have the right change, Pat, so I borrowed the money from your desk drawer. I'm returning it to you now," she explained.

---

5. "I sometimes have trouble talking to my mom at all," said Suzie. "She seems to have so many things on her mind, and she's always working so hard."

"My dad was the same way until the two of us went away together on a fishing trip," said Robert. "We had the best time ever. I'd never spent so much time alone with him before. We really talked. For the first time I could look at him as a friend."

			T	F	I

1. (A) Mimi's group doesn't know what country to report on.
   (B) Vickie is not a member of Mimi's group.
   (C) Students in the group must agree on what their report will include.
   (D) The members of Mimi's group already know some things about France.

2. (A) Drivers of cars with navigation systems do not need folded paper road maps.
   (B) A flashing light shows where the car is headed.
   (C) One compact disc can hold a road map for the world.
   (D) A person with a poor sense of direction will be less hesitant to drive to unknown places.

3. (A) Rhodes Scholarships are awarded for study at Harvard University.
   (B) Bonnie Saint John had her leg amputated when she was five.
   (C) To become a Rhodes scholar, it was essential for Bonnie Saint John to have had success on the college level.
   (D) Saint John won fourteen medals in national championships.

4. (A) Mother had borrowed Pat's money to pay the paper carrier.
   (B) Pat wasn't in the habit of locking the bedroom door.
   (C) Terry had taken paper from Pat's room.
   (D) Pat accused Terry of stealing money.

5. (A) The children want to spend time talking to their parents.
   (B) Suzie's mother has plenty of time to chat with her.
   (C) Robert and his father had gone on a fishing trip.
   (D) A trip for Suzie and her mother could help strengthen their relationship.

1.   The shad is a hard-fighting fish. A five-pounder can give a person a five-minute battle on rod and reel. Like salmon, shad return to their freshwater birthplaces to spawn (deposit eggs). When schools of shad leave the ocean to enter rivers, fishers take to small boats to troll for these fish. When a shad first gets hooked, a fisher may think the lure is snagged on an obstruction. But suddenly there are quick jerks on the rod as the fish leaps to free itself. Skill is needed to land and net a shad. To catch a female is luck indeed. Shad roe (the mass of eggs in her body) is considered a delicacy.

2.   A roadside directional sign in Lynchville, Maine, U.S.A., makes motorists think they may be dreaming. "Norway - 14 miles" reads the top line of the sign; then "Paris - 15 miles, Denmark - 23 miles, Naples - 23 miles." Touring drivers may well ask, "Is this a joke? Those places are all in overseas countries!" The rest of the sign is equally bewildering: "Sweden - 25 miles, Poland - 27 miles, Mexico - 37 miles, Peru - 46 miles, China - 94 miles." The sign is not kidding. All the places listed are actually towns in Maine or neighboring states.

3.   During a naval battle in 1841 between Argentina and Uruguay, the Uruguayans discovered that, though plenty of gunpowder remained, their cannonballs were almost gone! The captain of the Uruguayan fleet, desperately scanning the deck for help, noticed a stack of cannonball-sized objects. They were Dutch cheeses, too old and hard to eat. "Load them into the cannons!" ordered the captain. "Fire!"

The broadsides of cheeses wreaked surprising damage to the Argentine fleet, pelting scores of sailors and ripping jagged holes in sails. Argentina withdrew from the battle, leaving Uruguay the victor.

4.   According to a Greek myth, Echo, one of the loveliest of young maidens, fell in love with a handsome youth named Narcissus. Unfortunately, Narcissus loved only himself and paid no attention at all to Echo. In addition to this, poor Echo was punished, unjustly, by Hera, the queen of the gods. Hera denied Echo the power to speak except to repeat the last word or words of someone else. Imagine Echo's sorrow! Finally, she hid herself in a lonely cave. Although her body has long since wasted away, her voice still lives in caves and mountains, where it continues to repeat the last words of others.

5.   Michael Mirakian was shocked to hear of defenseless old people being mugged and robbed near the New York City high school where he taught. He realized that something had to—and could—be done. Mirakian's call for student helpers brought out four hundred volunteers. The students selected were assigned to centers for the elderly, where they began escorting old people to banks, stores, or doctors' offices and strolling with them through parks.

Besides aiding the elderly, the program produced bonuses for the teenagers involved. Often, their classroom marks and their outlooks on life improved.

UNIT 16

			T	F	I
1.	(A)	It requires skill to catch shad.	☐	☐	☐
	(B)	Shad return to their birthplaces to spawn.	☐	☐	☐
	(C)	Fishers find shad to be placid and easy-going fish.	☐	☐	☐
	(D)	Many fishers hope to catch a female shad before she deposits her eggs.	☐	☐	☐

			T	F	I
2.	(A)	The town of China is furthest from Lynchville.	☐	☐	☐
	(B)	Americans often name towns after foreign places.	☐	☐	☐
	(C)	Lynchville is located in the state of Massachusetts.	☐	☐	☐
	(D)	The places listed on the sign are towns in Maine or neighboring states.	☐	☐	☐

			T	F	I
3.	(A)	Sailors aboard the Uruguayan ships had not been starving.	☐	☐	☐
	(B)	The Argentine fleet was running out of cannonballs.	☐	☐	☐
	(C)	The Uruguayan fleet was running out of gunpowder.	☐	☐	☐
	(D)	The naval battle was won by Uruguay.	☐	☐	☐

			T	F	I
4.	(A)	Neither Hera nor Narcissus treated Echo well.	☐	☐	☐
	(B)	The Greeks made up myths to explain mysteries of nature.	☐	☐	☐
	(C)	A narcissist is a person interested only in himself or herself.	☐	☐	☐
	(D)	Narcissus was in love with Hera.	☐	☐	☐

			T	F	I
5.	(A)	Michael Mirakian was a New York City high-school student.	☐	☐	☐
	(B)	The volunteers came to realize the problems and fears that the elderly faced.	☐	☐	☐
	(C)	Students helped elderly people reach shopping and medical facilities.	☐	☐	☐
	(D)	Four hundred students volunteered to help the elderly.	☐	☐	☐

1.   One problem can become the solution to another. Problem number one was what to do with a huge old salt mine 650 feet below Hutchinson, Kansas. Problem number two was where to store piles of important old records and documents owned by government and businesses.

Some business executives hit upon the solution to both problems by leasing the salt mine. It has since become a mammoth storage vault for public and private records as well as for old TV films, hospital x-rays, and valuable books. Storage areas are bright, dry, cool, and wide as a highway. The mine is an ideal place to "salt away" old records.

2.   Consider the U.S. coins in your pocket or purse: are they what they seem to be? The penny, once ninety-five percent copper, now contains only 2.4% copper plating. The rest of it is zinc. The nickel is three-fourths copper and only one-fourth nickel. A dime minted since 1965 no longer contains silver; it has a pure copper core with nickel on the top and bottom; all three layers are visible. Newly minted quarters, half-dollars, and dollar coins are also composed of base metals, whereas older coins of these denominations were nine-tenths silver.

3.   "I saw the movie *The King and I* on television last night," said Doug. "It took place in a country called Siam, but when I tried to find Siam on a map, there was no such country!"

"I know why," responded Gretchen. "My sister Julie saved me a lot of time last night. She said that Siam is now called Thailand. That's not the only country with a new name. Do you think you would find Persia on a map now?" she added.

4.   Julio tried to look nonchalant as Karen closely examined the sculpture. Her critical eye took in the flowing lines of the horse's body, the suggestion of strong muscle under smooth skin. It was incredible; the animal looked almost real to Karen.

"This is magnificent," she said. "You should be very proud."

Julio smiled in relief. "Thanks, but I'll never be as good as you."

"Nonsense," Karen replied. "You have extraordinary talent. All you need is the training to cultivate it."

5.   Connors went to the window and looked out. The familiar landscape had an eerie look; gray ash covered everything like a shroud.

"The fire must be getting closer," he remarked. Then, almost as an afterthought: "Perhaps it's time to leave."

Connors moved toward his daughter. Her eyes showed her fear.

"Finish packing, Charlotte. Meet me downstairs. I'll have a hot cup of coffee waiting for you," said Connors as he picked up his carefully packed suitcase and walked toward the kitchen.

UNIT 17

			T	F	I
1.	(A)	"Salt away" means to store or set aside.	☐	☐	☐
	(B)	An old salt mine has been used to store records and documents.	☐	☐	☐
	(C)	The business executives couldn't solve both problems.	☐	☐	☐
	(D)	Paper will not soon decay in the mine.	☐	☐	☐

			T	F	I
2.	(A)	Today's U.S. coins contain more valuable metals than they formerly did.	☐	☐	☐
	(B)	Today's nickel coin contains three-fourths copper and one-fourth nickel.	☐	☐	☐
	(C)	Silver is too expensive to be used in newly minted coins.	☐	☐	☐
	(D)	Today's penny is made mostly of copper.	☐	☐	☐

			T	F	I
3.	(A)	Doug was unable to locate Siam on his map.	☐	☐	☐
	(B)	Gretchen had also wondered about the location of Siam.	☐	☐	☐
	(C)	Gretchen knows that Persia now has a different name.	☐	☐	☐
	(D)	Thailand was once called Siam.	☐	☐	☐

			T	F	I
4.	(A)	The horse Julio had sculpted looked almost real to Karen.	☐	☐	☐
	(B)	Karen told Julio he lacked special talent.	☐	☐	☐
	(C)	Julio valued Karen's opinion.	☐	☐	☐
	(D)	Karen urged Julio to train in a field other than art.	☐	☐	☐

			T	F	I
5.	(A)	Connors is able to stay calm in an emergency.	☐	☐	☐
	(B)	Charlotte was visibly frightened.	☐	☐	☐
	(C)	Connors is Charlotte's son.	☐	☐	☐
	(D)	Charlotte and Connors will lose their home to the fire.	☐	☐	☐

1.   Near Falls Creek Falls State Park in Tennessee there is a small A-frame vacation house that was built by a physically impaired person. Otis Pickett became paralyzed below the waist in an accident. Afterward he supported himself and his wife by making furniture and teaching woodworking. He began the house in 1972, working on it weekends for four years. Friends helped only with very hard work, such as pouring the cement floor and finishing the roof peak. Paneling, fireplace, walls, windows—all were done by Otis himself. For second-floor work, he hauled himself up by block and tackle.

2.   Jane Lehman became a skilled mountain climber when she was in her fifties and sixties. At fifty-one, Mrs. Lehman was tired, sickly, and allergy-ridden. Then, while watching a group of mountain climbers, she decided to try the sport. She trained by running up and down the stairs of the 555-foot-high Washington Monument with full backpack—seven times a day! Lehman has since climbed dozens of mountains, including fourteen-thousand-footers in the Rockies and Himalayas, and has been rated as one of America's best female mountain climbers. Her ills and tiredness have vanished.

3.   Many couples get married in places other than houses of worship. Chris and Leota Havens of Texas were married at the fast-food hamburger restaurant where Leota worked. There was no problem about what to serve at the reception. Larry and Liz Hedge were married "at home." Larry had a softball game in Wichita, Kansas, on the day of the wedding, so they tied the knot at home plate in the ballpark. Sam and Bridgette Money exchanged vows on a platform twenty-five feet above Omaha, Nebraska, and honeymooned three weeks in a tent up there—part of a radio-station publicity stunt.

4.   After winning the national outdoor junior tennis championship at fourteen, Maureen Connolly quickly achieved fame in adult competition. At sixteen she won the 1951 U.S. singles championship and repeated her victory in 1952 and 1953. "Little Mo," as she was nicknamed, also won the British title for three consecutive years and the French championship in 1953 and 1954. In 1953, she accomplished the "grand slam" of tennis by winning the Australian, British, French, and U.S. titles. Her career was cut short by a horseback-riding accident when she was nineteen. She died at the young age of thirty-four in 1969.

5.   Frank D. Peebles, Jr., chairman of the City Planning Commission, donated $300 to the city of Decatur, Alabama, when it celebrated its 150th anniversary in 1976. The money was put into a certificate of deposit, which, at 7.5 percent compound interest, will increase in value in the next 150 years to $21 million! The certificate was buried, along with souvenirs of the 1970s, in a time capsule to be unearthed in the year 2126. Then, said Peebles, the city can use the money for "parks, recreation, a cemetery, or whatever the city needs."

		T	F	I

1.
- (A) Pickett built an A-frame vacation home.
- (B) Pickett did not crave sympathy because of his misfortune.
- (C) Mrs. Pickett and friends helped Otis Pickett build the fireplace.
- (D) Pickett had very strong arms.

2.
- (A) Activity can cure some ills better than rest can.
- (B) By her sixties, Lehman was in better health than she had been in her early fifties.
- (C) Had Mrs. Lehman not decided to try climbing, she would still be ill and tired.
- (D) Jane Lehman became a famous mountain climber before she was ten years old.

3.
- (A) Guests at the Havenses' reception ate hamburgers.
- (B) The three weddings took place in Nebraska, Texas, and Kansas.
- (C) The Hedges were married at Larry's house.
- (D) Mr. and Mrs. Money honeymooned in a tent above Omaha, Nebraska.

4.
- (A) Maureen Connolly was nicknamed "Little Mo."
- (B) Connolly won the championships of four nations.
- (C) Connolly won her first national championship at age fifteen.
- (D) If not for the accident, Connolly might have been the greatest woman tennis player ever.

5.
- (A) Decatur, Alabama, was 300 years old in 1976.
- (B) Peebles was chairman of the board of a Decatur bank.
- (C) In 1976, Decatur, Alabama, received $300 from Peebles.
- (D) Peebles does not expect to be around in 2126.

1.   Our little friend across the street had been babbling happily to the neighbors about her upcoming birthday. Laurie is quite excited because she will be six years old and able to attend our local elementary school with her older brother and sister. All day today there has been a steady parade of children marching into Laurie's house. Each child is carrying a brightly wrapped package. One early arrival even dragged a huge bunch of balloons behind him.

---

2.   From the window of the plane, Bert could see the outline of mountaintops. Low-lying clouds covered some of the peaks. Bert's eyes opened wide as the plane flew between the jagged, snow-capped mountains. He could occasionally catch a glimpse of a lone hut or chalet nestled on a slope. Cows and goats grazed contentedly nearby. Every now and then the plane disappeared into patches of clouds. Bert could hardly wait for the plane to emerge into the sun again. The final descent began. A few minutes later, the plane landed in Geneva, Switzerland.

---

3.   Danny's parents had promised to buy him a new bike if his schoolwork improved. Consequently, Danny worked hard all spring. He also tried out for the school play, mainly because of his father's notion that there was more to school than academic studies. To Danny's surprise, he loved acting and became a great success in the play. By the end of the term all his grades had gone up. The day after the report cards came out, Danny saw a huge carton on the front porch.

---

4.   While vacationing in Austria, Louise and Irene Graff stopped at the home of their father's childhood friend, Herr Johann Dichter. As his wife, Frau Elsa Dichter, ushered the girls into the house, they could hear piano music in the background.
    "I didn't know that Herr Dichter was a pianist," commented Irene.
    The Graffs watched Herr Dichter at the piano. With many of the high and low notes they heard, the piano keys seemed to play by themselves. When the piece ended, Herr Dichter turned around and greeted them with a big grin.

---

5.   Every birthday for the past several years, Uncle Rob had given Rachel a crisp hundred-dollar bill as a present. This year, however, his business had taken a turn for the worse and he could afford only a birthday card. When Rachel saw the envelope in his hand, with her name written out in Rob's distinctive scrawl, she let out a whoop of delight. "Uncle Rob!" she cried. "You shouldn't have." To which her uncle replied, "Honey, I love you as much as ever. So let me caution you not to count your chickens before the eggs hatch."

1. (A) Laurie is an only child.
   (B) Laurie's birthday party is today.
   (C) Laurie has told her neighbors about her birthday.
   (D) The children going to Laurie's house carried bright packages.

2. (A) The sky was a mixture of clouds and sun.
   (B) The area over which the plane flew was heavily populated.
   (C) The plane landed in Switzerland.
   (D) Bert appreciated the advantages offered by the window seat.

3. (A) Danny did not work hard all spring.
   (B) Danny's new bike was in the carton.
   (C) Danny was able to participate in extracurricular activities and still get good marks.
   (D) Danny's father was proud of Danny's success in the play.

4. (A) Louise and Irene Graff were vacationing in Austria.
   (B) The upper and lower keys of the piano looked as if they were moving without being touched.
   (C) A mechanical player piano was providing the music.
   (D) Frau Dichter did not invite the Graffs into the house.

5. (A) Rachel was expecting another hundred-dollar bill.
   (B) Uncle Rob expressed his affection for his niece.
   (C) Rachel saw her name on the envelope.
   (D) Uncle Rob's business had been improving this year.

The story of Amelia Earhart, the woman aviator who disappeared over the Pacific while trying to fly around the world in 1937, has been told many times. Earhart might never have reached fame or known the joy of flying had she not met Mrs. Neta Snook Southern. Southern, a pioneer of early aviation, gave Earhart flying lessons.

Before World War I, Southern built her own plane so she could learn to fly. She may have been the first woman pilot in the United States. Later, she began barnstorming and giving airplane rides and flying lessons to the public in California. One day a Mr. Earhart brought his daughter Amelia for a lesson. The rest is history.

A. Exercising Your Skill

The passage is about Amelia Earhart and Neta Snook Southern, two female aviators who certainly could be described as confident, although that word isn't used directly in the passage. You can figure out that these two women were confident from their actions.

As you read, you will come across many characters who have confidence—and others who lack confidence, or are timid. You will be able to recognize these qualities in characters from information that the author states directly and from hints and clues in the characters' actions and conversations. Read the situations below. For each one, decide how a confident person might act or feel and how a timid person might act or feel. Write your responses on your paper.

Situations:

- a person your age who is new in the neighborhood seeing a group of other people your age walking together down the street
- a person who is about to try out for the first time for a school team
- a person your age who is giving a speech at a school assembly program

B. Expanding Your Skill

Continue working with details that tell about personality by creating word webs for the words *confident* and *timid*. Start out by drawing webs like the ones below. Then find words in the box that relate to either of the qualities, and add them to the webs.

sure	certain	follower	courageous	hesitant	shy
bold	fearful	doubtful	bashful	forward	leader

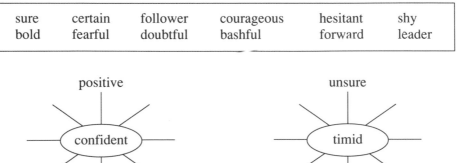

C. Exploring Language

Read the following situation. Then expand it in two different ways by writing two different paragraphs. The first paragraph should be from the point of view of José when he is feeling confident; the second should be from the point of view of José when he is feeling unsure. Give direct and indirect information about José in each paragraph you write.

You may want to organize the information for your paragraphs as follows.

Confident Character

Topic Sentence _____
    stated character detail _____
    suggested character details _____
    action details _____
Concluding Sentence _____

Unsure Character

Topic Sentence _____ _____
    stated character detail _____
    suggested character details _____
    action details _____
Concluding Sentence _____

Situation:

"Can anyone in the audience tell us the name of the British seaman who designed the ships that defeated the Spanish *Armada*?" piped the master of ceremonies. "Anyone giving the correct answer will automatically become a finalist in our Junior Scholars' Contest to be televised next week." "Do I know the answer to that question?" José said to himself.

D. Expressing Yourself

Choose one of these activities.

1. With some classmates, put on a puppet show for a group of young children. Plan for three or four main puppet characters. Have one puppet act especially confident and one act especially timid. Keep the plot of the story simple, and engage the puppets in plenty of action and in clear, simple dialogue.

   At the end of the show, ask the children what they thought of each puppet. See if they recognized that one character was confident and the other was shy.

2. Confident people have times when they feel unsure, and timid people have times when they feel confident. Think of a time when you have felt confident. Think of a time when you have felt unsure. Write about these situations. Include details about your actions, your thoughts, and how you imagine you appeared to others.

1. Janet was stretched out on her bed, her hands clasped behind her head as she stared thoughtfully at the ceiling. The lamp on her bedside table shed its studious light on the assortment of books and papers spread around her. Shortly, the early-morning light would creep through her window, but she was no closer to a solution than she had been at any time during the night before. All the clues were there, but her mind, usually so resourceful, could not seem to unravel them.

2. You've probably heard Sharon Michaels—though never her voice. She clumps, dances, and marches through the soundtracks of major films. It is her task literally to walk in the footsteps of such stars as Barbra Streisand and George C. Scott. When microphones fail to pick up an actor's footfalls, or when sound must be dubbed in after the filming of scenes, Michaels and her partner, Alice Clift, enter a recording studio containing various floor surfaces. As they view a soundless film scene on screen, the two women, wearing the appropriate shoes, match the actors' footsteps on one of the floor surfaces. Perfect split-second synchronizing of sound and picture is essential.

3. Mrs. Louise Sherwood, a senior citizen of West Virginia, tried to call her husband from the Cincinnati airport to tell him that her plane was snowbound there. Her poor hearing prevented her from distinguishing sounds. Voices weren't even audible to her over that phone.
    Once home, Mrs. Sherwood wrote to the United States Secretary of Transportation, suggesting that airports provide sound-amplifying phones like her home phone, whose sound level she can adjust with a small thumb wheel. Soon afterward, Mrs. Sherwood was notified that the Transportation Department was implementing her idea nationwide.

4. Anthony always had a great deal of difficulty getting up in the morning. Ever since he could remember, he had been roused from bed before the sun rose. Today was no exception. He dropped his leg over the side of the bed and pulled himself up to a sitting position. The varied barnyard sounds of early morning drifted in through the open window. The demanding bellow of the cows waiting to be milked resounded in his ear. This was still more pleasant than being awakened each day by honking horns and squealing brakes, Anthony reflected.

5. "Sometimes book characters seem very real to me," said Ali.
    "You're not the only one to feel that way," replied Sam. "Many people, for example, have believed that the character of Sherlock Holmes, created by Sir Arthur Conan Doyle, was real. Some have even gone so far as to search for his fictional home at 221B Baker Street," added Sam.

		T	F	I

1.
(A) Some of the clues were missing. ☐ ☐ ☐
(B) It would soon be light outside. ☐ ☐ ☐
(C) Janet does not give up on a problem easily. ☐ ☐ ☐
(D) Janet was stretched out on her bed sound asleep. ☐ ☐ ☐

2.
(A) It is not that easy to match a person's footsteps. ☐ ☐ ☐
(B) Alice Clift and Sharon Michaels can match actors' footsteps. ☐ ☐ ☐
(C) Sharon Michaels sings on the soundtracks of major films. ☐ ☐ ☐
(D) Sharon Michaels has literally walked in the footsteps of Barbra Streisand. ☐ ☐ ☐

3.
(A) Mrs. Sherwood could adjust the sound level of her home phone. ☐ ☐ ☐
(B) The Transportation Department became aware that many travelers are hard of hearing. ☐ ☐ ☐
(C) Mrs. Sherwood lived in West Virginia. ☐ ☐ ☐
(D) Mrs. Sherwood received a reply from the Transportation Department. ☐ ☐ ☐

4.
(A) The bellow of the cows was not the only sound Anthony heard. ☐ ☐ ☐
(B) Anthony had once lived in the city. ☐ ☐ ☐
(C) The sun had risen by the time Anthony got up. ☐ ☐ ☐
(D) Anthony had no trouble getting up in the morning. ☐ ☐ ☐

5.
(A) Ali likes to read fiction. ☐ ☐ ☐
(B) In the stories about Sherlock Holmes, Holmes lived at 221B Baker Street. ☐ ☐ ☐
(C) Sherlock Holmes was an actual person. ☐ ☐ ☐
(D) Sir Arthur Conan Doyle made his main character very believable. ☐ ☐ ☐

1.　For as long as she could remember, Yvette's parents had given her a rare coin to add to her collection on each of her birthdays. And for just as long, the young girl had looked forward to the gift.

But as she grew older, Yvette found that her interests changed. No longer interested in coins, she longed for a different gift, such as some new clothes. How disappointed Yvette was when her parents presented her with still another rare coin on her sixteenth birthday!

2.　No matter how hard she tried, Kellie couldn't see the movie screen in front of her. First she shifted to the right-hand side of her seat; then she moved toward the left. Finally, she asked the lady in front of her to remove her hat. But even after the lady did so, Kellie could not see the screen. "What am I going to do?" she thought. "No one else seems to be having this problem."

3.　Maureen shrieked in delight as the roller coaster hurtled downward and then swooped upward on its tracks at the county fair. "After this ride ends," she thought, "I'll go again."

But then, as the roller coaster ground to a halt, Maureen saw her parents beckoning frantically to her through a kind of haze from the midway. She noticed also that many people at the fairgrounds were running toward the exits. Now alarmed, the girl wrinkled her nose at the odor she finally detected.

4.　The pilot of the airplane had just moments to make a decision. Not far away, from the north, a vicious storm was moving toward the aircraft. In minutes the storm would strike, and the plane and its passengers would be in some danger for a short period of time. The pilot realized that beyond the storm lay peaceful skies where there would be no danger. She knew, however, that she could easily change her route to avoid the storm. That would be the safer course to follow, even though it would consume more time.

5.　Melanie struggled to pass the runners who were ahead of her in the race. As she ran, she thought of the many hours she had spent training while her mother always waited nearby to offer encouragement. Passing the other runners, she remembered also that her father had never appeared at her training sessions and that he wasn't among the spectators today. She knew that Dad worked long hours at his job. Even so, she wondered why he always seemed too busy to pay attention to the sport she loved so much.

			T	F	I
1.	(A)	Yvette's parents were unaware of her changing interests.	☐	☐	☐
	(B)	As she grew older, Yvette wished for new clothes rather than another coin.	☐	☐	☐
	(C)	Yvette's interest in rare coins began at age sixteen.	☐	☐	☐
	(D)	Yvette was disappointed when she received another coin.	☐	☐	☐

			T	F	I
2.	(A)	Kellie is not a very big person.	☐	☐	☐
	(B)	The woman in front of Kellie removed her hat.	☐	☐	☐
	(C)	Kellie would look for another seat with no one sitting directly in front of it.	☐	☐	☐
	(D)	Kellie was watching the live performance of a play.	☐	☐	☐

			T	F	I
3.	(A)	A fire had broken out at the fair.	☐	☐	☐
	(B)	Maureen's parents beckoned frantically to her.	☐	☐	☐
	(C)	Until the end, Maureen enjoyed her ride on the roller coaster.	☐	☐	☐
	(D)	Few people at the fair were running toward the exits.	☐	☐	☐

			T	F	I
4.	(A)	The pilot would avoid the storm and arrive late at her destination.	☐	☐	☐
	(B)	The storm was far to the south.	☐	☐	☐
	(C)	The pilot knew what was beyond the storm.	☐	☐	☐
	(D)	The pilot had to make a quick decision.	☐	☐	☐

			T	F	I
5.	(A)	Melanie's father and mother had different viewpoints about her involvement in sports.	☐	☐	☐
	(B)	Melanie passed the other runners with ease.	☐	☐	☐
	(C)	Melanie's father worked long hours at his job.	☐	☐	☐
	(D)	Melanie's father was at work today.	☐	☐	☐

1.   Mrs. Greason sat at the table looking out the picture window. She could see the children playing on the swings and the merry-go-round. Later in the day she would stroll over to the baseball diamond and watch the Little League practice. On Saturdays the baseball team usually had a game with one of the teams from a nearby town. Mrs. Greason never missed a game. She would sit right in the middle of the bleachers and cheer until she was completely hoarse.

---

2.   Edward tried not to look stunned as the waiter seated him at the magnificent dining table. The table was set with the best of everything: an exquisite lace table-cloth and the finest china, crystal, and silver that money could buy. The two hosts sat regally at either end of the table, partially hidden from each other by a bountiful arrangement of freshly-cut flowers.

Edward glanced at the bewildering collection of silver on either side of his plate. He would have to watch his hosts carefully to see which utensil they used for each different course.

---

3.   "This isn't nearly as bad as I thought it was going to be," said Marga with forced enthusiasm.

"You're right. It's distinctive," agreed Simone, trying to swallow.

Both girls were tasting a strange-looking dish that their host Miguel had insisted they sample.

"I told you you'd like our food once you tried it," he said.

"What is it?" asked Marga, almost afraid to hear the answer.

Miguel looked at her innocently. "Fried snake," he said, watching closely to see her reaction.

---

4.   The Apache chief Geronimo gazed in irritation at the small cloud of dust traveling at a snail's pace to the south. The remainder of his small warrior band stood in silence, hunger and fatigue evident on their faces. The group now numbered fourteen, including two scouts who must soon ride in search of the next campsite on their trip north. Two days at most and they would reach the relative security of the box canyon on the Rio Oro.

---

5.   Dolly and her family flew to a Caribbean island for a winter vacation. As the plane was landing, Dolly looked out the window. It was raining! But while they drove to the hotel the sun came out, followed by a rainbow. Every afternoon after that the sky would proceed to darken at 2 P.M. Then the rains would fall—hard—but only for twenty minutes or so. After that the sun would reappear. On the fifth day of her stay, Dolly was sitting by the pool when the sky darkened. She moved her towel to a shelter.

UNIT 22

			T	F	I
1.	(A)	Mrs. Greason could see the swings and merry-go-round from her picture window.	☐	☐	☐
	(B)	Mrs. Greason enjoyed living near the park.	☐	☐	☐
	(C)	From her picture window, Mrs. Greason would watch the Little League practice.	☐	☐	☐
	(D)	At the baseball games Mrs. Greason would cheer until she was hoarse.	☐	☐	☐

			T	F	I
2.	(A)	Edward was unused to formal dining.	☐	☐	☐
	(B)	The table setting was rough and simple.	☐	☐	☐
	(C)	Edward was unsure of how each piece of tableware was to be used.	☐	☐	☐
	(D)	The two hosts sat at either end of the table.	☐	☐	☐

			T	F	I
3.	(A)	Marga and Simone are guests of Miguel.	☐	☐	☐
	(B)	Miguel likes to surprise his guests.	☐	☐	☐
	(C)	Miguel told the girls they were eating fried snake.	☐	☐	☐
	(D)	The girls didn't particularly like the taste of the food.	☐	☐	☐

			T	F	I
4.	(A)	Geronimo and his band are being pursued by an enemy.	☐	☐	☐
	(B)	The Apache chief and his warriors are traveling south.	☐	☐	☐
	(C)	The Apaches estimate that they'll reach their destination—and safety—in two days.	☐	☐	☐
	(D)	Geronimo's band had dwindled to only fourteen warriors.	☐	☐	☐

			T	F	I
5.	(A)	On the fifth day of her stay, Dolly didn't count on the rain lasting long.	☐	☐	☐
	(B)	So far, the daily afternoon rains had fallen in gentle, mistlike drops.	☐	☐	☐
	(C)	Dolly was spending just a weekend on the Caribbean island.	☐	☐	☐
	(D)	Dolly saw a rainbow on the day she arrived on the island.	☐	☐	☐

1.   Several generations ago Ukranian immigrants settling in North Dakota brought with them a custom that survives today: the elaborate decoration of Easter eggs. Ukranian eggs are painted with complex designs in all colors and combinations. Many designs have symbolic meanings: the fish and the cross symbolize the Ukranians' religious faith; dots represent tears. The Ukranian artist works with four basic dyes and a special pen that writes with melted wax. Even though raw eggs are used, breakage is rare. The finished eggs are often preserved for years. Some North Dakota residents have eggs that were decorated and brought from Europe by their ancestors.

2.   According to a leading tire manufacturer, to find out whether your car tires have sufficient tread for safety, you can simply insert a U.S. penny into the grooves between treads. To test a regular-tire tread, hold the penny upside down with Lincoln's head facing you. If the top of Lincoln's head shows when the penny is inserted in the tread groove, the tread is overworn. Thus the tire is unsafe, so you should buy a new one. In addition, says the tire company, such a tire will give poor gas mileage, and you will have to use that penny—plus many more—at the gas pump.

3.   A hitherto-unknown species of shark was discovered off Hawaii in 1976—in a rather unusual way. When a U.S. Navy ship pulled in its sea anchor, the crew found a dead fourteen-foot, 1,650-pound shark with its teeth caught in the anchor. No such shark had ever been seen before. Instead of the familiar pointed snout and huge, razor-sharp teeth, this shark had a blunt snout and a huge, rubbery-lipped mouth with tiny teeth. Scientists were surprised also at the depth at which the shark must have been: five hundred feet. Apparently "Megamouth," as it was nicknamed, fed on deepwater plankton; thus it is not surprising that none of its species had ever been seen before.

4.   "Old stories tell about a mythical bird that died in flames and was then reborn from its own ashes," said the storyteller.
     "Wasn't that the phoenix?" replied Alex.
     "Yes," said the storyteller. "The phoenix was a character in the popular mythology of ancient Egypt and Greece. Because it was thought to go through endless cycles of death and rebirth, it became a lasting symbol of renewal," he added.

5.   Tigers live anywhere from twenty to twenty-five years. When a tiger becomes too old or too injured to hunt other animals, it may strike out at people in its path. One Bengal tiger living in India reportedly attacked two hundred people in a certain area of the country, then moved to another area to strike out at 234 more humans. According to another account, in one year tigers took the lives of 22,000 people in India.

UNIT 23

			T	F	I
1.	(A)	While decorating, a Ukranian artist handles the eggs with great care.	☐	☐	☐
	(B)	Only one color is used in painting Ukranian eggs.	☐	☐	☐
	(C)	Dots on the eggs represent tears.	☐	☐	☐
	(D)	Ukranian Easter eggs are not intended to be eaten.	☐	☐	☐

			T	F	I
2.	(A)	According to the tire company, there are two reasons for replacing overworn tires.	☐	☐	☐
	(B)	The tire manufacturer is telling about the penny test to prevent accidents and to sell more tires.	☐	☐	☐
	(C)	If a tread is overworn, Lincoln's beard disappears in the groove.	☐	☐	☐
	(D)	A tire with an overworn tread will give poor gas mileage.	☐	☐	☐

			T	F	I
3.	(A)	The shark was caught by sailors with a rod and reel.	☐	☐	☐
	(B)	The shark had an extremely large mouth.	☐	☐	☐
	(C)	There may be other undiscovered species in the world.	☐	☐	☐
	(D)	The shark was nicknamed "Megamouth."	☐	☐	☐

			T	F	I
4.	(A)	The myth of the phoenix still interests people.	☐	☐	☐
	(B)	Many ancient Egyptians and Greeks had heard stories of the phoenix.	☐	☐	☐
	(C)	The phoenix was believed to die by drowning.	☐	☐	☐
	(D)	The phoenix of mythology died and was reborn again and again.	☐	☐	☐

			T	F	I
5.	(A)	Bengal tigers are found in India.	☐	☐	☐
	(B)	Young tigers are interested more in killing other animals than in killing people.	☐	☐	☐
	(C)	A single tiger has been known to kill more than 200 people.	☐	☐	☐
	(D)	Tigers have a life span of about fifty years.	☐	☐	☐

1.   "See the world's biggest pig and the brainiest rabbit!" cried the barker in the flashy suit. "For just a dollar you'll see two living wonders."

Ella and Martha looked at each other. "That sounds interesting," said Martha. "We've already gone through most of the other exhibits at this fair."

The girls each handed the barker a dollar and went in.

"This rabbit doesn't seem very smart," said Ella.

"I've seen bigger pigs than that one on my uncle's farm," said Martha. "Let's get out of here."

---

2.   Keith was ironing his shirts in his basement. Suddenly he remembered that he had to pick up his suit at the cleaners. He put down the iron, jumped into his car, and drove toward the cleaner's shop. "I hope I get there before closing time," thought Keith.

Keith reached the shop in time, got his suit, and drove home. As he neared his house, he saw a fire engine. Then he remembered.

"Oh, no!" cried Keith. He jumped out of the car and raced toward one of the firefighters. "What's burning?" he shouted frantically.

"Nothing's burning," answered the firefighter calmly. "The fire engine is stopped here because it has a flat tire."

---

3.   When the state of Rhode Island celebrated its 350th anniversary in 1986, hitherto-unpublicized historic facts were brought to light, including a reference to the city of Newport's newspaper, the *Newport Mercury*, which had been established in 1758. Ann Franklin, the sister-in-law of Benjamin Franklin and a printer like Ben, published the *Mercury* and in 1762 became its first woman editor. (When her husband James had died in 1735, Mrs. Franklin had carried on his printing business.) The *Newport Mercury* is still the oldest continuously published newspaper in the U.S.

---

4.   "I've heard a lot about Bigfoot," said Suki, "but not about the yeti. Do you know anything about it, Aunt Tori?"

"Yes, Suki. The yeti is also known as the Abominable Snowman," replied Aunt Tori. "It is supposed to be a big, apelike creature that walks upright like a man. It is thought to live high in the Himalaya Mountains of Asia. A British mountaineer claimed to have photographed yeti tracks in 1951, and many Himalayan villagers claim to have seen the yeti, but there is no definite proof that the yeti really exists."

---

5.   Experts are investigating the cause of an explosion at a local factory. They aren't certain whether it was caused by leaking gas or by dynamite. Some of the machines in the factory are powered by gas. A spark could have caused the gas to explode. The factory also had dynamite stored in its basement, which was against the safety rules. Fortunately, the explosion occurred on Sunday.

			T	F	I
1.	(A)	Martha and Ella were annoyed that they had been tricked into the exhibit.	☐	☐	☐
	(B)	The barker claimed to have the world's most intelligent pig on exhibit.	☐	☐	☐
	(C)	Martha said she had seen bigger pigs on her uncle's farm.	☐	☐	☐
	(D)	The price of admission for the exhibit was one dollar a person.	☐	☐	☐

			T	F	I
2.	(A)	Keith went to the cleaners for his suit.	☐	☐	☐
	(B)	Keith was ironing his own shirts.	☐	☐	☐
	(C)	Keith thought he forgot to turn off the iron when he put it down.	☐	☐	☐
	(D)	The firefighter said that Keith's house was on fire.	☐	☐	☐

			T	F	I
3.	(A)	Ann Franklin was the first editor of the *Gazette*.	☐	☐	☐
	(B)	The state of Rhode Island was 350 years old in 1986.	☐	☐	☐
	(C)	Aptitude for printing and publishing was characteristic of the Franklin family.	☐	☐	☐
	(D)	The *Newport Mercury* is still being published.	☐	☐	☐

			T	F	I
4.	(A)	Some people believe in the yeti without real proof.	☐	☐	☐
	(B)	Bigfoot is known as the Abominable Snowman.	☐	☐	☐
	(C)	No one has yet come face-to-face with a yeti.	☐	☐	☐
	(D)	Aunt Tori knew more about the yeti than Suki.	☐	☐	☐

			T	F	I
5.	(A)	Some machines in the factory are powered by gas.	☐	☐	☐
	(B)	Experts are trying to find the cause of the explosion.	☐	☐	☐
	(C)	The explosion couldn't have been caused by dynamite.	☐	☐	☐
	(D)	Workers were not in the building.	☐	☐	☐

1.   Grated nutmeg adds a special flavor to many foods. Have you ever sprinkled it over hot or cold milk drinks or used it in baking or with fruits? Nutmeg is a spice that is also used to flavor meats and sausages. Before it is grated, the whole nutmeg is oval or round—the dried seed of the nutmeg tree. This seed has a lacy covering from which another spice, called mace, comes. In the countries of Grenada, Trinidad, Malaysia, Indonesia, Sri Lanka, and Singapore, workers can be seen separating nutmeg and mace.

2.   The authorship of "Mary Had a Little Lamb" has generally been attributed to Sara J. Hale—who published it in her *Poems for Our Children* in 1830—though her authorship is sometimes disputed. Left a widow with five children to support, Mrs. Hale devoted herself to a literary career. She wrote fiction, edited the *Ladies' Magazine* of Boston, and later edited *Godey's Lady's Book* of Philadelphia, which greatly influenced the fashions and manners of her day. She was an outspoken advocate for higher education for women and for a national Thanksgiving holiday. Sara Hale lived from 1788 to 1879.

3.   In 1899 the steamship *Stella* left Southampton, England. Nearly two hundred passengers were aboard, bound for holidays in the Channel Islands. A fine mist crept over the sea, then turned into a dense fog. The ship crashed into rocks and began to sink. Lifeboats were lowered, and a stewardess, Mrs. Mary Rogers, helped passengers into them. When it was discovered that one woman had no life belt, Rogers took off her own belt and gave it to the woman. Refusing to get into an overloaded lifeboat for fear of sinking it, Mrs. Rogers called, "Goodbye, goodbye!" Moments later she and the ship sank beneath the waves.

4.   Charmian Orpen Hill, who grew up in Ireland in the 1920s and 1930s, was the only member of her family who liked horses. She became a proficient rider at an early age, then married and raised four children. At forty, Hill was able to resume her riding career, becoming a jockey. When she became a grandmother, she received the nickname "Galloping Granny." At sixty-one, Hill began racing the horse Dawn Run, which she and her son had purchased. Although Hill retired from racing in 1982, the talented Dawn Run went on to win the Cheltenham Gold Cup in 1986.

5.   "What's your favorite Dr. Seuss book?" Dad asked after he had finished reading aloud *The Sneetches.*
      "*Horton Hatches the Egg,*" replied Amy without a moment's hesitation.
      "I still like *The Cat in the Hat* best of all," said Lee. "I laugh every time I read it."
      "There's no doubt that Dr. Theodor Seuss Geisel is a popular author," said Dad. "The two of his books that I'd choose over all the others, though, are *Yertle the Turtle* and *One Fish, Two Fish.*"

T F I

1. (A) Grated nutmeg makes eggnog taste more special.
    (B) Nutmeg is the dried seed of the nutmeg tree.
    (C) Mace comes from the covering of the seed.
    (D) Nutmeg and mace are different names for the same spice.

T F I

2. (A) President Lincoln was influenced by Sara Hale when he proclaimed Thanksgiving a national holiday in 1863.
    (B) *Godey's Lady's Book* was published in Boston.
    (C) *Poems for Our Children* was published in 1830.
    (D) Mr. Hale did not leave his widow and children a fortune.

T F I

3. (A) The wreck of the *Stella* remained on the rocks for years afterward.
    (B) Passengers aboard the *Stella* were on vacation.
    (C) The memory of the brave stewardess remained with the passengers she had helped.
    (D) The *Stella* was going from Southampton to the Channel Islands.

T F I

4. (A) Charmian Orpen Hill acquired her interest in horses from her family.
    (B) The Cheltenham Gold Cup is a prestigious award.
    (C) Mrs. Hill became a jockey at forty years of age.
    (D) Mrs. Hill and her son purchased Dawn Run.

T F I

5. (A) Amy's first choice of a Dr. Seuss book is *The Cat in the Hat*.
    (B) Dad said that Dr. Geisel is a popular author.
    (C) The children's dad had finished reading aloud *The Sneetches*.
    (D) Dr. Seuss sometimes liked to give his books humorous titles.

Anthony always had a great deal of difficulty getting up in the morning. Ever since he could remember, he had been roused from bed before the sun rose. Today was no exception. He dropped his leg over the side of the bed and pulled himself up to a sitting position. The varied barnyard sounds of early morning drifted in through the open window. The demanding bellow of the cows waiting to be milked resounded in his ear. This was still more pleasant than being awakened each day by honking horns and squealing brakes, Anthony reflected.

A. Exercising Your Skill

In the passage above, you learned that Anthony would prefer to hear cows bellow than to listen to horns honking and brakes squealing. He has seemingly made a choice to live in the country rather than in the city. In your reading, you will often learn what characters prefer or value through directly stated information or through hints in what they say or do. Think about what some of your preferences are. Write each topic below as a heading on your paper. Then write your own preference under it.

Food	Type of Movie	Recreation Spot	Way of Traveling
Sport	Type of Story	Weather	Place to Do Homework

B. Expanding Your Skill

Compare your preferences with those of some of your classmates. Were some choices similar? Why do you think some were and some were not? Now think about some of the things you do when you prefer one thing over another. On your paper, write each word or phrase from the box under one of the following headings:

<u>Things Preferred</u>　　　　<u>Things Not Preferred</u>

wrinkle nose	shake head	frown	ignore
put thumbs up	nod head	cheer	smile
move toward	put thumbs down	laugh	boo
spend time	avoid	hiss	clap

C. Exploring Language

For each of the following circumstances, continue the story by telling about a character making a choice. Include direct information as well as clues about the character's preference.

- "For a new girl at school, I really feel at home," Dana said to one of her new friends. "I've been invited to two parties over school vacation, and Lisa invited me to go to the science museum with her and her cousin. I have a decision to make, though," Dana went on. "My 'old' best friend, Gwen, has asked me to spend the week with her back in my old neighborhood."

  _____

  _____

  _____

- Mike was leaning against the fence, waiting for his friend Luis to meet him. When Luis arrived, he said, "My father just told me about a TV special that's coming on in an hour. It's that one we heard the guys talking about yesterday at school. Do you still want to play ball, or do you want to go to my house to watch the program?"

  _____

  _____

  _____

- "Look at those two strangers snooping around the Randolphs' backyard," said Jan to her roommate Pat. "Should we call the police right away, or should we try to find out who the strangers are?"

  _____

  _____

  _____

D. Expressing Yourself

Choose one of these activities.

1. Conduct a poll of your classmates to find out their preferences. Use topics listed in activity A or choose others. After you have collected the information, analyze it to see if any preference trends show up. Work with other students to report the poll results. Write a Report of Class Preferences.

2. With a partner, make up a skit in which two characters disagree about a choice that has to be made. Include information about each character's point of view in the script. Present the skit to a group of classmates. You and your partner should use both verbal expression and body gestures to add emphasis to each character's point of view. At the end of the skit, ask your classmates to decide which character made a more convincing argument.